By PAUL METZLER

Fine Points of TENNIS

8493
796.34
M

STERLING PUBLISHING CO., INC.   NEW YORK

Oak Tree Press Co., Ltd.   London & Sydney

BY THE SAME AUTHOR

Advanced Tennis
Getting Started in Tennis
Tennis Doubles
Tennis Styles and Stylists

CONTENTS

INTRODUCTION

Organized so that each item, complete in itself, fits into the whole fabric of the game of tennis, this book is written so that you can go straight to what you want to know without any build-up. Detailed explanation of grips, for example, is in the Appendix.

Emphasis is on playing your best tennis in a match, and the book starts off with developing a match temperament. You must know what to do almost automatically to win a match without doubt or hesitation, and the advice given, along with plenty of practice, should enable you to gain the confidence you need to win.

Also recognizing your opponent's skills and weak points is necessary to succeed in competition, so a large part of this book is devoted to opponent analysis. You will eventually find that every player fits into a known type.

Left-handers, there's special information for you, but elsewhere you can read left for right. As for you women, your game is really no different from men's so where the player is identified as a man, it could just as well be a woman. The awkward entanglements of saying "he or she" have been avoided, but not because of male chauvinism.

PAUL METZLER

"Airlie,"
12 Buena Vista Avenue
Mosman, New South Wales
Australia 2088.

1. MATCH TEMPERAMENT

Perhaps you'd give your right arm to have good match temperament. It won't come about by a miracle, but it *will* come through work. You're more than willing to work, of course, but how?

The first thing to do is to find the *core* of match temperament and separate it from such facets as the will to win, etc., which you know you can handle any time you try. *The core of match temperament is feeling confident that you can hit the shot you're playing.*

You object that that's far too physical, whereas your real trouble is mental; it's nervousness. All right, we'll turn to nervousness at once.

Nervousness

This not only ruins your game but even before you have played, it has interfered with your sleep and almost certainly with your lunch. Many players say they eat a light lunch so that they won't feel over-burdened, but often the truth is that eating any more would choke them. Years ago, tennis champions were thought of as remote beings with nerves of steel or no nerves at all. Nowadays, we see some of the best tennis in the world being played by players who admit to being nervous. Yet they have excellent match temperaments.

Setting that aside, you'd like to be rid of your own nervousness. Besides butterflies in your stomach, you have wooden feet, blurred vision, shaky hands—and even the racket handle feels like a pick-axe.

You can settle that last one at once. In your nervousness you grasp the handle hard down in the butt of your hand and it feels uncomfortably thick. So, hold it in your palm and fingers, as you do when you're not tense. (See Illus. 1.)

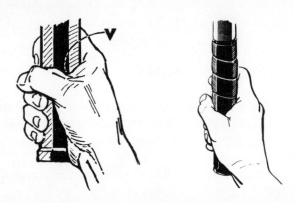

Illus. 1. RACKET HANDLE FEELS THICK. Both are Eastern forehand grips, with the V in the center of the top surface. But they can feel as differently as they look—left clumsy, right comfortable.

And when you first walk onto the court, even if it's a familiar one, always feel its surface with your toes and feet. Feel it distinctly—and then you'll have feet in your shoes instead of two lumps of wood. All your shots, remember, are mounted from your feet.

Nervous blurred vision comes from closeness. You're looking at the ball only after it bounces and shoots at you. Look beyond the opposite back fence, look at your opponent, look at the ball coming to you the whole way and therefore slowly. If it's still a little blurred in the early stages of the game, you can still hit it—because if you can see a ball well enough to dodge one coming straight at your face, you can see it well enough to hit it. Even if you are almost sick with nervousness, you can always hit the ball—and no one notices that you look any different.

If you *are* physically sick, which is unlikely, get it over and done with. Tell your opponent you're sorry and that it must have been something you ate—then take a piece of chewing gum or a peppermint and get on with the game. If you're sick in the dressing room just before the match—why, that's doing it in comfort. It has nothing to do with your subsequent match temperament, when you're playing the ball.

Look at it this way: if your opponent told you he'd felt ill in the dressing room—something he ate—you wouldn't suddenly expect him to be as weak as a kitten in the match, easy to beat.

Shaky hands and twitching stomach cannot stop you from playing your shots. Try it in a practice set. Practicing, you can't make yourself feel nervous, but you can shake your hands about, and then satisfy yourself that you can still throw the ball up and serve properly.

Although you can play through these physical effects you can't stop feeling nervous, so you needn't bother trying. Nervousness itself is built into all of us.

Nevertheless, a few things can help. However you feel as the match is about to start, take a vow that you won't lose while still feeling physically cold to any degree and that at least you'll work hard. Throughout the match, watch the ball, hit the center of your strings and hold onto the ball, and play firmly. Know exactly what you ought to be doing and try to do it without doubt or hesitation. And be clear-headed enough to recognize your opponent's type of game—because he's showing it to you.

But worth more than all that put together, you'll agree, is that match temperament core: to feel confident that you can hit the shot you're playing, and get it in. If you can achieve that, you must have a good match temperament—whether you're nervous at the start of a match, or when you fall behind, or when someone important to you arrives to watch you in the middle of your match and makes you feel self-conscious, or near the end when victory and perhaps title are within your grasp. Also, your nervousness may disappear, but whether it does or not there's no doubt that your match temperament will be good.

Match Temperament's Association with Strokes

You weren't born with a good or bad match temperament. In general, your match temperament is directly connected with the confidence you have in your strokes at the time you're playing them; in particular, it varies with each different stroke. Think over the following examples.

You have a grooved and steady backhand and a faster forehand that is often wayward, and you're playing a baseline rally for a vital point. Six shots come to your backhand and you play each one firmer than the last—your match temperament is like a rock. If these balls had been on your unsound forehand, your match temperament would probably have broken down.

You always seem to lose close matches, and decide that you have poor match temperament when the chips are down. But how did you lose? Ten to one it was not the fault of one of your better strokes.

You led 5–4 and only had to serve out the set. You failed, through tightening up on your serve. You wouldn't have tightened up like that if your serve had been sound and you felt confident of attacking with it. Instead, probably your main thought was to avoid disgracing yourself by serving a double fault when victory was in sight.

You lost your last match on the easiest of balls, twice. You held match point and forehand-volleyed a high and fairly slow ball across court and over the sideline. Later, your opponent had match point, and you did the same thing, over the other sideline. Two easy balls at match points—and you felt uncertain with both. Because you have poor match temperament? No. Poor technique.

You do not play your high forehand volleys well, or you would not have felt uncertain, twice. It's likely that you play them from square-on to the net, and that when you had match point you hit across the ball. With high volleys, slide your left foot well forward and also put your left hand up if you have time, and then hit exactly along the line you have set up for yourself. You can't miss, even if you're feeling excited and nervous; and it doesn't matter in the least whether you have a killer instinct or a quiet and retiring disposition.

With the second match point—the one you missed to your off side—from square-on you pushed your wrist forward, the ball hit your racket below center and it popped up and over the sideline. (See Illus. 2 on next page.)

You're a brilliant young shot-maker, but you break down in matches and get beaten when everyone expects you to win. You've heard people talking about temperament losing more matches than strokes ever won, and you decide your whole trouble is that you have poor match temperament. What's more, you can prove it: your strokes are good, until you're in a match; the only different factor is the match; therefore you have poor match temperament and that's all there is to it.

You can take ten marks for simplicity, but you may as well say that when you subtract one from two you indisputably get one, and that that's all there is to mathematics.

It's your groundstrokes that break down. Probably you make last-second contact and are never "on" the ball (racket coming forward in line with ball for as long as possible). As for holding onto the ball, you've probably never heard of long contact in your life.

Acquiring Good Match Temperament

The important thing is to work on your strokes, making them sounder and sounder—sound enough to give you good match temperament. Take an interest in ball control.

The strokes most closely connected with match temperament are long ones: second serve, forehand and backhand. Develop a second serve that can be a double fault only when you decide to risk something extra with it; develop a forehand that you can roll in eleven times out of ten; and a backhand that feels *solid*, because you know it's going to be attacked.

Whenever you lose when clearly you should have won, don't blame yourself. Pin-point the stroke culprit—there's sure to be one. Be sure to pin the right one, though, even if it's your

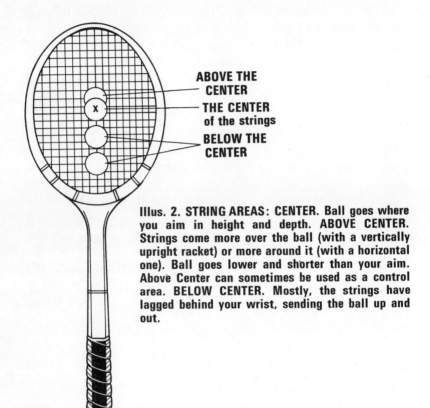

ABOVE THE
CENTER
THE CENTER
of the strings
BELOW THE
CENTER

Illus. 2. STRING AREAS: CENTER. Ball goes where you aim in height and depth. ABOVE CENTER. Strings come more over the ball (with a vertically upright racket) or more around it (with a horizontal one). Ball goes lower and shorter than your aim. Above Center can sometimes be used as a control area. BELOW CENTER. Mostly, the strings have lagged behind your wrist, sending the ball up and out.

favorite because you play it exactly like some champion. Grip, swing, even characteristic body movement—you've imitated the star player down to a T. But the contact between ball and strings cannot be the same, or he wouldn't be a star and you a player with poor match temperament, coming from an unsound stroke.

Other Facets of Match Temperament

You can cover these aspects mainly by understanding and determination.

ATTITUDE. Don't be one of those reluctant match players who feels he can't play well in heat or cold or wind, or on a fast or slow surface, or with a certain brand of ball, or against a certain type of player or even a certain type of person. Don't let thoughtless bad manners upset you, or interruptions or even bad calls. Take pride in adopting the attitude that *nothing* can put you off your game. It becomes interesting to see how well you can maintain it.

WILL TO WIN. Everyone starts with it. During a long match it often slips away unnoticed, particularly if you begin to feel satisfied with your efforts so far merely because you've given your opponent a good game. Even if he is a well-known player, you should be sharply aware that the end of the match may look a long way off to him. Remember that you enjoy playing, even if long and grimly.

CONCENTRATION. You don't have to concentrate continuously for every second of the time that the match embraces. But you do have to concentrate continually on every point of it. It is not enough to concentrate well for most of the points, because you may pay a high price for a few lapses. If you concentrate well and win the first set 6-1 and lapse on a point or two that gives your opponent a service break and the second set at 6-4—for that short lapse you're right back where you began.

SELF-PITY. Recognize it.

TEMPER. The spelling alone warns you that it's part of temperament. If you must lose it now and then, don't lose concentration with it. Whenever you go into a blind rage or a red haze, start ball-watching most consciously. You may imagine that you have an uncontrollable temper, but it is far easier to control anger than to shed nervousness.

HATING YOUR OPPONENT. If you're certain it strengthens your

play, go ahead and hate him. But if it makes you worried about losing to such an unlikeable person, don't force yourself to hate even a hateful opponent.

KILLER INSTINCT. If you like that term, be a killer. But don't feel deprived of anything if it doesn't suit your nature. Determinedly piercing your opponent's weakness with your strongest shots will take its place.

General Temperament

You're high-strung, excitable, indecisive, under-confident, pessimistic—or whatever else it is. Take another glance at self-pity and another good look at the core of match temperament, and then decide that you can be a tennis player after all. And that you can enjoy it.

2. NET GAME

Playing a net game means coming to the net on all first serves and most second serves, playing a serve-and-volley game. Taking the net continually, sometimes behind your serves but more usually from approach shots, is all-court tennis. Making only occasional net sorties (for surprise or when you're on a certainty) is baseline tennis, not all-court; strong volleying from the net does not make it a net game.

NET COVERAGE

With the net game there's no surprise in your position. Your opponent knows you will be there, in a better position to play the ball than he is, if you can reach it. To you, reaching it is crucial.

Therefore, the essential thing is not that you can punish a high ball severely from close to the net, but you can *cover* the net. You have to be "hard to pass" and "hard to get over."

The serving and volleying of successful net players catch the eye; their net coverage is less noticeable. However, many a strong server and volleyer finds that although he successfully plays net-game doubles he can't play net-game singles. When he makes sure of covering passing shots he gets lobbed over. He just cannot cover both. He hasn't got net coverage.

At times net coverage appears to consist of quick reflexes and agility and at others of high and wide reach, but in fact its two main elements are position and anticipation, which go largely unnoticed.

POSITION

Following in on your serve, your position is mainly concerned with covering a passing shot to either side. After you've played your first volley and moved in, your position is a combination of the *center of possible returns* and *lob cover*.

First Volley

Serve in good balance and move in quickly, *but without rush.* Never rush or charge the net—that's not balanced net play. Move in swiftly and smoothly, feeling *balanced.*

You'd like to get well into the net, but that's not possible. You'd still be advancing while your opponent was hitting the ball, and you'd have poor court coverage.

Follow in along the line of flight of the ball, trying to get as far as you can before your opponent hits it, and call yourself too slow if you don't reach to about the service line. Wherever you are, slow down there, pause. Don't regard that as a handicap, but rather see yourself as being poised to volley well, building a two-stage advance and making yourself a hard player to pass.

Then play your first volley, of whatever height, with your weight moving forward. When it's a wide volley get what forward weight you can by aiming your front foot towards the net post rather than towards the sideline.

Move in.

Second Volley, Perhaps Smash

If you've volleyed straight ahead towards your opponent's center, move straight in. If you have volleyed to either side, move in and towards that side—to the instinctive area that is in the center of possible returns and not too close to the net. (See Illus. 3-4).

Illus. 3. (opposite page) CENTER OF POSSIBLE RETURNS. That's it, in diagram. In play, give mental priority to protecting against down-the-line, where it's easier for your opponent to hit. Crosscourt is more difficult for him because he has to hit the ball across your body and beyond your reach, and yet keep it inside the sideline. The closer you position yourself to the net the more difficult his crosscourt becomes—but see Illus. 4.

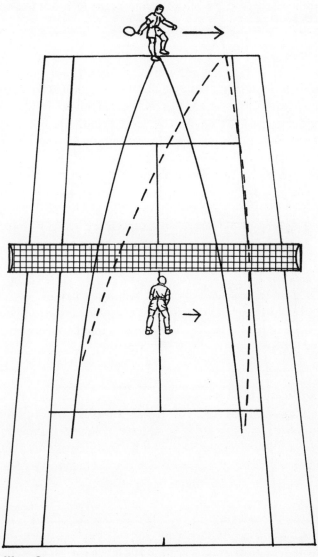

Illus. 3.

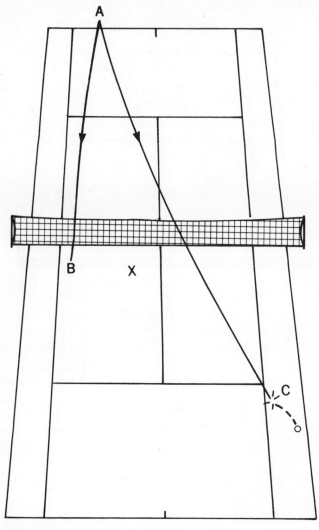

Illus. 4.

How Close?

Move in no more than a couple of steps if your volley is short. Your opponent is going to attack you, and you will need time to cover his shot or perhaps even to get your racket in place if he hits straight at you. If you close right in to narrow his angle you will move straight under a lob lifted over your head. Back from the net you'll have to low-volley and perhaps half-volley, but that can't be helped. Don't play your first volley short next time.

Move in no more than halfway between service line and net if you have volleyed deep, because he'll probably lob in reply, but be ready to move closer if he prepares to drive.

Go well in if you have volleyed into his shoelaces and he's tangled up and will have to hit a defensive half volley. You should also be in this close position if he throws his weight forward and hits out strongly with a heavy topspin dipping half volley. If this shot is a backhand it is almost certain to be hit with outside topspin, across and over the ball, and its direction will be crosscourt towards your backhand volley side.

Go right in if your volley has skidded wide. Your opponent will only be scratching to play it over the net, without enough strength to lob.

From these guidelines you should be able to get your own feel of the seven yard area that lies between service line and net. Let this feel for your position vary with different types of opponent. Star players seem to be able to do everything from a little closer to the net, but it's their net coverage you must emulate rather

Illus. 4. (opposite page) LOBBED OVER. While still covering down-the-line AB, the closer you move to the net the less room your opponent has to play his crosscourt AC beyond the reach of your forehand volley and land it in court. If you move right up to X as shown, for AC to be out of your reach it will have to land out. But you'll be lobbed over.

than their position. Don't merely look aggressive, and get lobbed over.

For subsequent volleying, move from one position to the next smoothly, almost as part of your shot's ending.

Too Far Back?

You can easily tell if your general net position is too deep. You're playing from too far back if you're forever low-volleying and never getting your share of volleying down; too far back if your game always includes more half volleys than anyone else's.

You're too far back if your opponents can roll fairly deep crosscourt shots across your body and into court almost as easily as going down the line. You need to make them risk playing sharper angles than that. You're too far back if an opponent can see too much of your court, because you don't put any net pressure on him. Then he can take his time without minding how many of his shots you cover.

Being a hard player to pass or get over doesn't mean you have to be timid. The net game demands cover but it is based on attack and not on defense. You may tell yourself that you can always move in closer against a high ball and make a high volley, but continually playing from a position only about a yard inside the service line is scarcely an attacking attitude.

Overprotecting against lobs makes you hang back too far. Stay there, and no toss ever comes. It's better to base your protection on reasonably good lobs, not on the perfect specimen. You should be far enough back to protect only when a lob is likely, and that is practicing the art of anticipation.

ANTICIPATION

If you have good position, and are well-versed in the art of anticipation you can make your opponent feel not only that you're hard to pass, but that your racket is almost magnetic.

To achieve this you must move into position at the instant he is committed to his shot but fractionally before he hits it.

Move earlier, and he changes his direction or his shot; move later, and you're passed.

There are more ways to anticipate shots than just noticing how an opponent may unknowingly telegraph the direction of his shots. Here are various anticipation techniques, in increasing order of difficulty to apply:

Forcing your opponent to play the shot you expect
Inducing his shot
Reading his telegraphy
Recognizing his preferred direction
Influencing his choice of direction

Forcing a Shot

You serve wide to the right court and receive a backhand volley. Your placement of this volley practically forces a shot you can anticipate. (See Illus. 5 on next page.)

Lob. You play your volley BC behind your opponent as well as wide. If he's going to be able to do anything else but toss, you'll see this well before he gets to the ball.

Low Crosscourt. Play BD with slice, sending the ball and its bounce wide and low for a scrambled return that won't have enough strength for a lob. Your opponent's down-the-line shot would also be weak and easily covered, so his best chance is to play very low over the center strap, hoping you might wobble a low volley into the net. But you close in, as he's committed, and volley easily into an open court.

Tangled Shot to Your Backhand Volley. Expecting you to play BC or BD he sets off at good speed, and BE tangles him. Whether he plays his backhand half volley fast, to hit himself out of trouble, or quietly, it will be easier to hit over and around the ball and direct it towards your backhand volley side. Don't move early, letting him change his mind from a

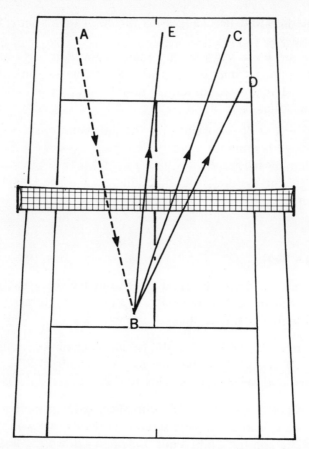

Illus. 5. FORCED ANTICIPATION. AB is the service-return, volleyed at B. BC is deep to bring a lob, BD sliced wide to scramble him, and BE played into his hurrying feet to bring another shot to your backhand side.

direction that you're ready to cover. Let him commit himself first, then move. Even if it's a lob, you're ready to move to your left and you'll cover it with your forehand overhead.

Your opponent seems to have more options in this last example, but on court your BE is an almost errorless shot and his reply is often a nothing shot.

Inducing a Shot

Neither of you has done well. Your opponent lost his balance in returning your serve and your first volley luckily went awkwardly somewhere under his right arm. You've moved in and he's not in balance to hit a strong shot.

He'll choose to toss over your backhand side, because that's what you'd do if you were there. Stay where you are and induce him to carry on with it—then cover it. Move back and left, hitting a forehand smash to your off side from beyond your left shoulder if need be.

If you move back too early he can stay in the game by doing little more than pushing the ball into play. (See Illus. 6.)

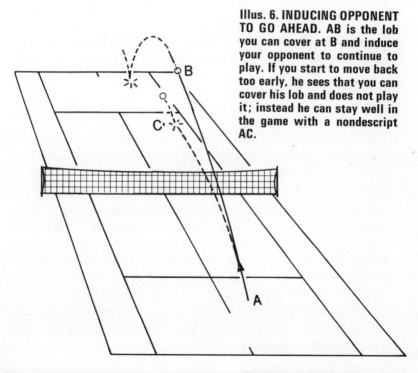

Illus. 6. INDUCING OPPONENT TO GO AHEAD. AB is the lob you can cover at B and induce your opponent to continue to play. If you start to move back too early, he sees that you can cover his lob and does not play it; instead he can stay well in the game with a nondescript AC.

Telegraphy

- He lines himself up in the direction he's going to hit his shot, telegraphing its direction.

- He drops his racket head lower than usual on the backswing. He's going to lob.

- On the forehand he moves his left (front) shoulder and left leg farther across. He's going to pull the ball crosscourt.

- On the backhand he places his right (front) leg well across and almost turns his back to the net. He's going to hit down the line.

- Between his crosscourt and down-the-line shots on both forehand and backhand, he "somehow looks different."

- He normally slices his backhand, but when he winds up for a hard topspinner he always hits around the ball as well, and sends it crosscourt.

- He's a left-hander who looks relaxed rolling his forehand crosscourt to your backhand, but you can see him setting himself up when he's going to hit in his less natural direction down the line.

Anticipation relies heavily on such telegraphy against all sorts of opponents. They can try to disguise their shots and they can try to second-guess you by hitting in the opposite direction after deliberately telegraphing, but they cannot keep hitting in unnatural directions all the time with success, any more than you could. They can fool you now and then when they have plenty of time—but seldom indeed when hard pressed, because of the likelihood of making errors that give you the points directly without your needing either anticipation or volley.

When you are preparing to serve at love-all in the first set against a new opponent, be well aware that you already have a good idea of what he "looks like," from the warm-up. You can't help observing him.

PREFERRED DIRECTION

Many a player's preferred direction is completely obvious if you look for it. Such a player will always use that direction when he is trying under pressure to pass you and when he has a chance to make an outright winner past you. You simply have to wait for him to commit himself before you move.

There also are less obvious indications. For example, most right-handers play their forehands better when hitting away from their bodies, to the offside. This comes from a past tennis history of having played hundreds of balls towards an opposing right-hander's backhand and only dozens towards his forehand. This preference may not be overwhelming and is often only marginal, but with most players it's there.

Few players' forehand stroking is so pure that they swing in a straight line from hip to hip, playing down the line or cross-court merely by pointing their hips. Most play down the line by swinging their arms somewhat away from their bodies and play crosscourt by swinging across their bodies. This difference is accentuated when you're at the net and they need to steer a ball down the line or pull it abruptly crosscourt. You can't help noting which shot such a player makes better, which he will prefer at some time when you have nothing else to guide you.

Crosscourt Preference

Picture now, if you will, the service returns of a couple of doubles players. One is a right-hander who always hits a strong outside-topspin crosscourt forehand drive from the right court, and the other is a left-hander who plays in similar fashion from the left court. You can easily recognize this type of player (right-handed or left) when he plays singles, and can expect him to have a crosscourt preference with his passing shots.

Backhand Direction

Preferred direction with the backhand is simpler. For the normal topspin and the downward-sliced backhand it's crosscourt and for dropped-head inside-spin backhand it's down the line.

Running Crosscourt

There's another type of preferred direction, not associated with a player's stroke-making action but with the situation he's in.

In the example of running crosscourt drives in Illus. 7, your opponent is trying to turn defeat into victory. You've served to his backhand in the left court and then volleyed across to his deep forehand corner for a likely winner. But he runs hard across the baseline and reaches the ball in time to make a fast topspin drive for an intended outright winner. He realizes that if you're able to volley the ball he'll still be leaning against the side fence. Assuming his shot is perfect, all depends on whether you can anticipate down-the-line or crosscourt.

As shown in Illus. 7, he is likely to go crosscourt from A and down the line from B. In reality he's hitting the ball genuinely crosscourt from A and "crosscourt down-the-line" from B. Anyone running hard across to a wide ball gets a better feeling of control when he hits around the ball (crosscourt direction), and has a fear of spraying it wide into the doubles court in hitting to the off side. From B, "crosscourt down-the-line" is more easily played than the wider and more exacting genuine crosscourt.

NOTE: You see champions sometimes hitting down the line from A and on the run, but most players miss as often as they succeed. Therefore, when you're in this position yourself, it's better to play percentage tennis and hit crosscourt, because there are plenty of opposing net players about who aren't likely to know that you will not be aiming down the line.

To help you cover the court against a fiercely hit shot from either A or B, go in as far as you dare, to reduce the angles open to your opponent. Blocking them completely will take

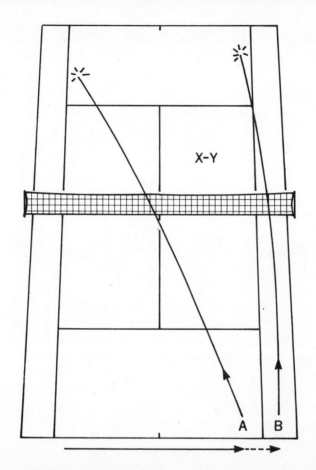

Illus. 7. RUNNING CROSSCOURT DRIVES. Both shots have been HIT as crosscourts. X and Y are positions in the center of possible returns from A or B. A is within its sideline and B outside it.

you too far in and at once make you look like a warning lighthouse. Then, although he'd been prepared to drive hard he'll lob for an easier winner.

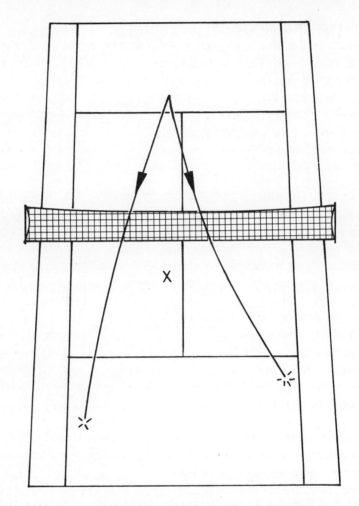

Illus. 8. LOOKING DOWN THE GUN BARREL. Your only chance is to influence your opponent's direction.

INFLUENCING DIRECTION

Illus. 8 is meant to portray a position where you're down on your beam ends. There's been an exchange of shots, with your opponent doing the attacking, and now he has you set up for a forehand drive kill. The ball is above net height and not deep, and he can pass you cleanly on either side without telegraphing his intentions or using his preferred direction or anything else. Your last resort is to influence his direction and then cover that side in a flash.

NOTE: Bouncing up and down in the same spot is useless and swaying widely from side to side is ridiculous. You may be swaying right when he hits left—though that's unlikely, because swayers always stop their waving about before the ball is hit, making it all pointless. Be alert and poised to move without display—or onlookers may think you're trying to balk your opponent unfairly, and raise a derisive cheer when he does pass you. Never play your tennis like that.

You can leave one side more open, *marginally* but almost imperceptibly so that your opponent will not know you are aware of it. Otherwise he will second-guess you and wrong-foot you by playing into the smaller opening, or else he'll hit well wide into the too-wide opening you've invited him into. In leaving one side fractionally more open it is usually better to choose the crosscourt side (your forehand volley side), in the hope that if he perceives what you're up to and hits wide he *may* pull the ball over the sideline as well.

Or, in imperceptibly influencing his choice of direction, you may move across into your best net position in the center of possible returns just a little slowly or a little late, but fully prepared to spring farther across when he takes the bait and commits himself to the direction you choose for him.

Or, you can appear (again almost imperceptibly) to have anticipated too soon. Lift your right knee a fraction, turn your right shoulder another fraction, lift your racket a third one— all as though you're going to volley on the backhand. Then spring across for a forehand volley on your "unprotected" side, before he hits the ball but while he is committed to this direction.

If you're successful, most onlookers will think that you showed lightning reflexes and supreme agility; perhaps a few ungracious ones will believe that you picked the right direction by sheer luck. From your opponent's viewpoint, you're a heartbreaker.

Anticipation doesn't work all the time, but there's no such thing as a good net-game player without it. Whether you are gifted with a basic sense of anticipation or not, there's no substitute for experience. A knowledge of all aspects of anticipation greatly aids this experience.

3. NET GAME SHOTS

SERVE

To keep your head up while you serve is what beginners are told. But if you drop it in your hurry to get moving towards the net you won't see the ball *continuously*. And that's important to a net-approaching player.

Your service concept should be to serve an attacking ball, with both first and second balls, which you follow to the net to take advantage of. You cannot play the net game feeling that you are going to the net on a short ball, or trying not to serve a double fault.

Therefore, your serve should feel automatic, going automatically over the net and automatically dropping in—with you as the gunner firing this automatic weapon and advancing.

The ball will never go consistently over the net without a good net clearance. That varies with your own height and the speed of your serve, but average figures are about two feet for your first serve and three for your second. Net skimmers clear the net beautifully in practice sets or in matches against weaker opponents. In close matches and finals, however, they refuse to live up to their name and hit the tape instead. Your match temperament varies greatly with the normal net clearance of your serve.

After a safe net clearance the ball needs to drop, so visualize your serve's flight as an arc. (See Illus. 9 on next page.)

Topspin-Sliced Serve

Such an arc is available to you, by means of a topspin-sliced serve. Its mechanics produce a curving arc, one that you can aim. Today it is the most generally used serve. See Illus. 10, comparing this serve with its two better-known ancestors.

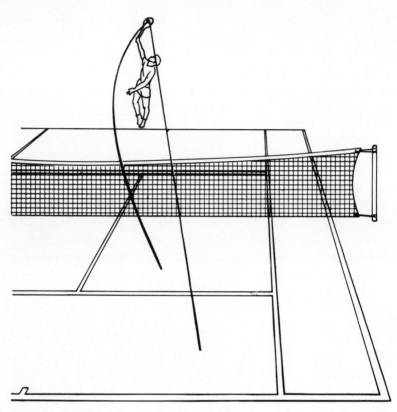

Illus. 9. SERVICE ARC. Imagine what it does for your match temperament.

Sliced Serve

The sliced serve needs a lower net clearance to land in court. It has a wide curve which aids serving wide of the receiver's forehand in the right court, and perhaps aceing him; but with a second serve intended for the backhand your opponent has every chance of stepping around the ball and attacking you with his forehand. To find his backhand you have to curve the ball well over the wrong side of the net band, as in Illus. 11 (on the next page), and on an important point that can be nerve-wracking.

Nevertheless, the sliced serve is the best serve of all against an opponent who cuts or slices his service returns, because its low bounce prevents him from hitting the ball downward with good passing angles. Instead he has to hit the ball up. His slice, unlike a topspin shot, travels fairly straight instead of dipping into court and is easy to volley.

Topspin Serve

The topspin serve, and especially its extreme version, the American Twist or kicker, arcs the ball severely and allows the highest net clearance. However, it has accompanying dis-advantages. You lose speed and also you are more likely to

Illus. 10. TOPSPIN-SLICED SERVICE. It gives a safer net-clearance arc than the Sliced, with more speed and better variation of direction than the Topspin.

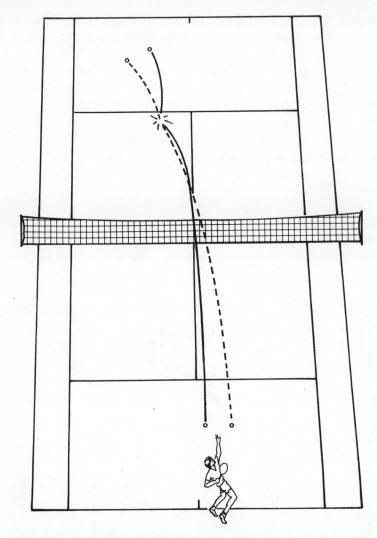

Illus. 11. THE TOPSPIN-SLICED is fairly automatic for a second ball to the backhand in the right court. With a Sliced serve even its bounce favors the receiver's forehand. Also you have to risk aiming well over the wrong side of the net-strap, and then if you falter the ball lands in the wrong court. The Topspin-Sliced is better for your peace of mind.

Illus. 12. CANNONBALL OR FLAT SERVE. It's not really flat, but is hit with a trace of slice, or else the racket face comes over the ball and gives it a trace of topspin. However, trying for great speed, most players lose some of their follow-in balance. Also, it has less drop than other serves and so demands a lower net clearance, and thus it cannot be regarded as an "automatic" serve. It is an occasion ball, not a stock ball.

mis-hit. Although the ball is naturally directed to a right-hander's backhand, the heavy spin you apply reduces your accuracy in placement. The high bounce of the ball opens wider angles for your opponent's passing shots. The high arc gives you more time to follow in for your first volley, but this is largely offset by your being out of balance at the end of this service and immediately before you begin to follow in.

With the topspin serve, both your racket and your right leg finish out to your right side. The sliced and topspin-sliced serves, on the other hand, finish with the racket to the left of your body, carrying your weight forward, and your right leg is stepping forward into court as the first step of your net approach. The two latter serves give you a more coordinated and smoother net advance.

Nevertheless, the topspin serve has its uses. A receiver with a weak backhand hates it. Against a stronger type of player, you can greatly reduce the number of difficult topspin drives your opponent can make as his service returns, which you would otherwise have had to meet with your first volley. Why? When confronted with a high-kicking serve to his backhand, even a player with a good rolled backhand in normal play prefers to play a more easily-made backhand slice—and with a topspin serve you're nearly always serving to the backhand.

Flat or Cannonball Serve

For a time the flat or cannonball serve was popular and all very good servers included it in their range. (See Illus. 12.) Now they seem to have discarded it, to a large extent because it wastes too many first balls. For any two points it is usually better to serve two topspin-sliced first balls into play than one cannonball and one second ball.

Your Own Serve

Illus. 13 shows the generally accepted ball positions for the sliced serve (to the right and in front of your right shoulder) over to the American Twist (above your left shoulder). However your own topspin-sliced serve doesn't need to conform exactly to any diagram. It's the feel that counts, the feel of the ball-and-strings contact that makes you serve a topspin-sliced ball, if that is what you want.

You may prefer your sliced serve with its snappy curve, or your topspin one with its reliable arc. But do get an automatic feeling with it. Comparatively few points are won by service alone, but rather by the service/first-volley combination that consistently solid serving sets up.

American Twist

Topspin or Flat

Topspin Slice

Slice

Illus. 13. SERVICE BALL POSITIONS. They're average positions, diagrammatic ones, and not necessarily yours because they vary with the action each server uses. A few people serve nearly flat from the American Twist position and regard the Topspin position as their sliced one. Their opposites put topspin on the ball from the Sliced position (throwing it somewhat farther back) and for their Sliced serve they throw the ball farther forward and perhaps lower down. Average or unusual, it's the feel that counts.

Let's say you have a fast first service that goes in once out of twice. That's not bad; at 30-all all you'd have hit is two fast first balls in. But when this fast first serve misses, and your second ball is not difficult, your opponent begins to count on this and always attacks you from it. He's not supposed to be attacking as often as half the time. You're the one who's playing the net game.

And whenever it's 30–40 or ad.-out there's big pressure on you to get your big serve in. You're playing your match temperament again—through one of your strokes.

It's far harder for your opponent if he finds himself continually attacked—with a first serve of good speed or a second one that is slower but carries more spin. And behind either one there you are all the time, making a first volley and closing in. It gives him no peace.

Grip (see Appendix 1)

Use the Continental grip. The racket handle is not in the same line as your forearm, meaning that your wrist never impedes the butt of the handle and you can serve freely.

After serving, your racket is in the same grip that you'll probably use to play your first volley.

Left-Handed Serving

If you're left-handed, make the most of it. Right-handers dislike your serve, saying either that it cramps them or that they don't know where it's going next. They take great comfort from a left-hander who misses a lot of first serves, appreciating the extra time the slower second ball gives them to sort out its left-handed kinks.

You can readily see your advantage in having a more or less automatic serve that allows a high percentage of first balls. You direct them and the receiver doesn't like them. The outlook for comfortable first volleys is good.

It is a great asset if you have a strong sliced serve from the left side that swerves wide of the receiver in the left court and fairly spreadeagles his backhand. Don't be dismayed, though, if such a serve is not natural for you; fewer left-handers have it than fearful right-handed receivers imagine. Instead, concentrate on cramping your opponent. He will find that nearly as bad.

Foot-Faulting

As a net-game server you are likely to foot-fault practically all the time if you are unaware of it.

Some net-game foot-faulters seem to have three feet, all foot-faulting. They move the front one forward and foot-fault, then drag the toe of the rear foot past their front foot and foot-fault by more. They make yet another forward movement with the first one—and then hit the ball, after foot-faulting three times for one serve. Their net advance is rapid, and unfair.

When you are called for a foot-fault, position yourself a little farther back for your next serve, but do not let this make you feel either that your serve will be short or that your net advance will be impeded. Settle down and feel *normal*.

Never lose your concentration by getting annoyed with the official who called you. That won't happen if you understand beforehand that most foot-fault judges don't enjoy calling foot-faults; it's their duty, but they feel like spoil-sports, interrupting the game. When umpires are responsible for calling, they hate it. Against a young player they feel bullying; against an old one, rude; one of their own age, smart; a teammate, disloyal; an opposing team player, unsporting; and a visiting champion, presumptuous and embarrassed.

Still, it's best avoided. When anyone shouts, "Foot-fault!" it can sound to you like an accusation of unfair play, at best a caution. One thing's certain: your serve is a fault.

When practicing, take the trouble to see how your service action moves your feet, and then always make allowance for it.

Illus. 14. LOW BACKHAND VOLLEY. See yourself as being set like this, a picture of a player who can't miss. He looks compact, firm, strong, balanced, natural, and intent on the job at hand.

VOLLEYING

Expect your volleying to be sound. There are two good reasons why it can be. The obvious one is that your shot is played from nearer the net than when you hit a serve or groundstroke, and the other is that a volley needs only a short action, and thus is a stroke that is easy to play in good form.

A perfectly produced stroke is not just a coach's model; in match play it gives you an accompanying feeling of firm safety. It seldom misses.

For example, volleying with a horizontal or parallel racket (meaning wrist and racket head are *about* the same height above the court) is not merely nice-looking form but also gives you the greatest safety margin for any possible error in your timing as you punch forward to meet the ball. In direct contrast, if you volley a low ball with a vertical or perpendicular racket head you only have to come forward a fraction late for the ball to go too low and into the net, or a fraction too early for it to go too high and over the baseline. In like manner, volleying with a dropped racket head (meaning, racket sloping downwards at an angle of about 45 degrees to the ground) reduces the safety margin your shot could have had. Clearly, good volleying form equates with soundness and confidence.

Now, please see Illus. 14 and the list of praiseworthy points in its caption.

Analyzing these points:

● Any well-played backhand volley lends itself to a compact appearance. The pictured player heightens this effect because he happens to have his wrist held snugly near his knee.

● The stroke looks firm because the wrist is held firmly back instead of weakly bowed forward.

● The right foot is strongly placed, giving forward weight.

● The player's balanced look comes from his bent knees and straight back; if he played with straight knees and bent back he'd look rocky.

● The most natural-looking volley you can play is about waist high, where it's completely natural for you to volley with your racket about horizontal. In playing a ball that is somewhat lower than waist high, our player has brought his waist down to about the ball's level.

● His head is inclined downwards, not left up in the air, but with eyes intently on the ball.

● And he looks as though he can't miss, because in conjunction with everything else he has turned well sideways and he has the ball covered with a horizontal racket, which allows him the greatest margin for any timing error.

Volleying Grips (see Appendix 1)

Use the Continental grip, if you're effective enough on the forehand side with it. For the first volley, you've got the grip you've just served with and the best one for handling low and wide balls. Closer to the net, there's no change of grip between forehand and backhand—and if that's an advantage in making rising-ball service returns against fast serves it goes double for rapid volleying.

If your Continental forehand volley feels weak, use the Australian forehand grip, probably making a small change for the backhand.

If either of those forehand grips feels weak (neither has your palm solidly behind the handle), at least be prepared to use the Australian for wide volleys and for low volleys forced on you very quickly. But concentrate on making time to use your Eastern forehand volley (which needs to meet the ball farther in front) whenever you can. Never lower your own effectiveness, and your match temperament along with it.

If you're a Western-style player on both forehand and backhand your net game is at a disadvantage. To volley the ball either flat or with the more usual slight under spin you have to meet the ball well in front of your body, and this gives you less time to make your shot or cover a wide ball than any other style of volleying does.

First-Volley Constant Error

Various strokes have their most usual or most natural error, normally termed Constant Error. With lobs, it's playing too short; with smashes, it's hitting down into the net; low volleys, the net; high volleys, over the sideline; etc. But since first volleys come at any height and angle and also at varying distances from your body, you may not have noticed that this mixed bag can have its own constant error.

It's lack of application.

Every player knows that if he misses his first volley there won't be any others, and that as far as the point is concerned (though not his confidence) he may as well have served a double fault. Yet many who purposefully finish off a point after an exchange of shots or fight hard to keep it alive, refuse to scramble for a difficult first volley and seem to miss even medium ones fairly complacently.

You won't lack application if you serve each time with that concept of serve/first-volley combination in your mind. Get into the habit of playing all your first volleys in. When practicing or playing against weaker players, experiment or fool about with some other shot, not this one.

Low Volleys

The easiest place to hit a low volley is into the net. Many a player does this in the first stage of all his matches, before he adjusts, but even after that many low balls are difficult to get over.

Particularly with a forehand volley, remember that your Continental grip opens the face of your racket (racket face tilts slightly upwards) and that this aids you in playing the ball over.

A fast and *very* low ball often feels too heavy for your normal low-volley stroke to be able to play the ball over the net, no matter how strongly you hold your wrist. Against these demanding balls play your volley with the frame of your horizontal racket right down on the court's surface, in contact with it. This gives your wrist wonderful support against the heavy weight of the ball.

To make a very low backhand volley that you can't meet well out in front, don't tie yourself down to always using the Continental grip. Use the Australian forehand grip as a backhand volley grip.

When your opponent's shot is heavily sliced, make sure you volley it over the net. Such a ball runs fractionally down your short strings and rebounds from your volleying racket somewhat lower than you think. If you don't use enough lift, a slow, heavily spun ball can wobble dismally into the net.

Players who bang low volleys against fast drives straight back over the net and the baseline as well, have no feel. The cause is holding the racket handle hard against the butt of the hand. You should feel such volleys with strong but absorbing fingers, and with your palm as well. There's no light daintiness in that.

Although you have a good feel for volleying, you can unexpectedly volley over the baseline against a fast drive with heavy topspin. The ball rolls fractionally up your short strings and rebounds a little higher than normally.

Wide Volleys

Can one grip be the most open and also the most closed?

Yes. For hitting a forehand volley within easy reach the Continental gives the most open racket face and the Western the most closed. However, the opposite holds true for a wide ball. The Continental allows you to volley round a ball that the Eastern could do no more than volley straight ahead, and the Western could volley only away to the off side. With reference to your long strings, the Continental is the most closed grip and the Western the most open.

Feeling that you can get round most wide balls instead of merely behind them does wonders for your net coverage.

As a second conundrum, can your racket face be open and closed at the same time?

Yes, and you make good use of it. When you're wide, you're weaker and the ball needs a little more lift. You get that from a "short-strings open-faced racket," most easily with the Continental grip. Against a very wide and low ball you get round the ball (with long strings closed face) and at the same time you lift it (with short strings open face)—so you're using a closed-face racket and an open-faced one at the same time.

It's far simpler, though, to call this Continental specialty an open-faced hook. (See Illus. 15.)

For maximum reach on the backhand use an Eastern forehand grip as a backhand volley grip, keeping your wrist back and bringing the racket face around the ball. Turn *well* sideways, turning your back to the net, and step out widely with your right leg.

Illus. 15. OPEN-FACED HOOK. For a ball that's wide, low and behind you use an extreme Continental grip. Intentionally use your right leg, too. It gives you wider reach, and also your open stance helps to lift a very low ball.

Ability to get around the corner in this way on both forehand and backhand seems to give you a volleying reach like a six-foot Eastern-grip player or a seven-foot Westerner.

Medium Volleys

Since you can't expect your opponent to return your service badly most of the time, take good advantage of a medium-height volley when you serve for your serve/first-volley combination. You've served to the right court, steadied at the service line; the ball is not fast and will give you a medium volley on your forehand. Good.

Play with a bit of flair. Step smoothly forward, bend your front knee, glide your racket *slightly* under and inside the ball and send it and its going-away bounce into your opponent's deep backhand corner. Move in.

There's no carelessness in any of that. The point's more safely in your keeping than if you carefully bumped your volley over the net, carefully well into court.

Volley well in front of your body, for solidity and a very good view of the ball. Even if you play your game with an Eastern forehand drive and a Continental volley, volley farther in front. It stops you from cutting the ball too much, thereby losing power and perhaps mis-hitting as well.

The easiest place to hit a medium volley is into court. This is easier than intentionally hitting the tape or missing the backline by less than a foot, where your errors usually go.

High Volleys

Against a slow ball a high volley is an easy shot with several feet of net clearance available to you. Never miss it.

Again, volley well in front. Line yourself up by sliding your front foot well forward. On the forehand, put your arm up if there's time, *watch the ball* and hit the center of your strings instead of looking somewhere ahead.

A high volley against a fast ball is often missed. This mostly happens when the player volleys with a vertically upright racket, either because he has to from the position of the ball or because that's his normal way of hitting a high volley. No shot better exemplifies the danger of having only a small margin for error in timing when playing a fast ball.

It's highly unsound to take much backswing when you're hitting with a vertical racket. Most players don't against a fast ball, but some always feel that a high ball is there to be hit, and they hit it. It's only about even money whether they hit a winner at great speed or crack the ball over the sideline or even the baseline.

Even if you take little or no backswing, make sure, when playing with a vertical racket, that you don't push your wrist too far forward. This tilts your racket face back slightly; that's fatal against a high fast ball and your shot goes out. It's a common error.

Stroke-volleys, in which you stroke the ball rather than punch or block it, are not thought to be as safe as more orthodox volleys. At least they don't induce playing with a vertically upright racket.

Feeling Stronger When You Volley

It's generally accepted that the Continental is the weakest of all forehand grips for hitting the ball forwards. However, if you realize that your Continental forehand volley grip is sometimes a closed grip (when you are getting around the ball) this should make it feel stronger to you than formerly. Also, the Continental is the strongest grip of all against the racket twisting in your hand when the ball doesn't strike the exact center of your strings.

If you're an Eastern-grip volleyer on the forehand you probably feel that your backhand volley is decidedly the junior partner. Realize that for the same short-length blow a backhand action is stronger than a forehand one, provided you're not leading with the back of your hand.

The backhand volley is made more quickly, too. With your racket somewhat across your body and cradled in your left hand, your fastest reflex action is a backhand volley. You use it to volley fast balls hit straight at your body, and should try to protect even your vulnerable right hip with it.

Angle or Depth for Volleying

Usually play your first volley deep.

● Beware of angling a low volley over the sideline.

● Don't angle wider than you need to.

● Don't angle to a position from which you can easily be passed.

Other than that, do not restrict your game by avoiding angles because they're supposed to be dangerous. Volley for depth or angle, whichever is more sensible at the moment.

If you have a general preference, either for the way you volley or the way you like to attack, use it. You're more effective that way. You're playing your strength, and one hopes your opponent dislikes it.

If you're a strong volleyer you may like to volley strongly and safely deep to the baseline—feeling that you're powering your opponent towards his back fence, from where all his shots will be long, giving you more time to deal with them. Or, it may suit your game better to volley strongly for the sidelines, somewhere between the service line and the baseline, and have your opponent run wide to cover your volleys. Play your preference and you'll be right.

Similarly, if you volley with more control than strength you may like playing angles that are almost out of your opponent's reach, and have him continually scraping for the ball, unable to generate enough power for his passing shots to worry you. Or, you may have a solid overhead game and regard deep volleying as the instrument you use to make your opponent toss.

Use your own method to get what you want, and you'll get it. For instance, if you've heard of a net-game player who is renowned for his solid smashing and you go to see him play, you won't find that his opponent shuts this renowned shot out of the game by never playing a lob. Your player will still be smashing much more often than the average player does. He volleys for it.

Illus. 16. LEFT-HANDED VOLLEY. Low wrist, racket head up, weight going forward—STRONG shot.

You're a Left-Handed Volleyer

Most left-handers play doubles from the left court, developing effective service returns with a long swing on the forehand and a very short one on the backhand. If you carry this stroking imbalance over to your volleying in the middle of the court, it doesn't give you the same effectiveness. Instead it often results in a somewhat erratic forehand volley and a rather weak backhand volley. If that applies to your game, shorten your forehand volley for more solidity and lengthen your backhand (but not by much) for more weight to it. For your backhand crosscourt volley, at the very least, keep your wrist low and your racket head up. Set yourself up as shown in Illus. 16 for as many volleys as you can.

Be aware of your natural advantages too. Most right-handers' preferred direction for their passing shots from both forehand

and backhand is towards your forehand side, where you have your wider reach and better shot. Also, many right-handers do not anticipate the direction of your left-handed volleys nearly as well as they anticipate a fellow right-hander's volleys, and that makes their reaction much slower.

HALF VOLLEYS

The Case For

A half volley is part of your stroke range, not a makeshift shot you've been forced to play.

Against a very low ball it's better to play a half volley from the center of your strings than to play a very low volley that hits their lower side. You're in better balance to merge into your next net position from a comfortable half volley than when you stretch forward to the last inch to volley, and stumble forwards after doing so.

As for hooking around a very wide ball, you have more time to play a half volley because you meet the ball a little later in its flight. Your net cover becomes very wide—octopus arms.

Very low volleys are heavy work, whereas the natural spring of the ball makes many half volleys feel effortless.

When you're moving in after your serve and the return is shorter than usual, it's far better to play a smooth en route half volley and move in than to backpedal and snatch at a rising ball. When leaning back you've often got your head up in the air, on the forehand side anyway, and you don't watch the ball. You're badly balanced to get into your next position (you'd never merge into it) and it's farther away than it need have been. Net-advance backpedalling is only done against a short slow ball, from which you can make a strong shot.

The Case Against

If you can half volley well, the greatest trap is over-indulgence. You cover wide balls without haste, and that natural half-volley spring of the ball makes much of your play easy. It's most pleasant to live in Lotus Land.

There are penalties. Immediately, your play becomes mild, and then, inevitably, sloppy. You lack penetration, because no one's half volley has the accuracy for angling or control for depth that his volley allows him. Balls that you could have played with a knee-high volley, you allow to land down at your feet.

That's the worst place they can be. The main thing against all half volleying is not the difficulty of the stroke itself but the position of the ball. It's right down on the ground, and needs to be lifted over practically the whole of the height of the net and then kept in court. You can cope with that all right, but when this ground-level ball is straight in front of your feet you have to use probably the least effective shot you possess.

You're forced to use a vertical racket, which gives you the least margin for timing error. In addition, you must play with your eye-level as far away from ball-level as it can be—and that gives you your worst sighting.

You shoot a rifle with your eye-level at the sights; and you couldn't aim as well if it were down at your feet. Standing straight up and half volleying from your feet (when you needn't have been in that situation) is like shooting at ankle-height from choice.

Playing Half Volleys

Although it means lifting the ball a little more, play your half volleys from as close to the ground as possible. This makes your timing much easier and avoids the mis-hitting or partial mis-hitting that accompany many late half volleys. And playing the ball close to the ground makes you go for it, preventing you from hitting it reluctantly and faltering. A half volley rises more than you imagine, so you *must* go for it early.

Second, play all the half volleys you can with topspin

Illus. 17. BACKHAND HALF VOLLEY. The racket has not yet hit the ball (which rises higher than you think). From a very short backswing, the racket face will roll UP and over the ball in follow-through. Direction will be crosscourt.

follow-through—like a "half drive" rather than a "half volley." (See Illus. 17.)

It's not possible to play half volleys close to your feet with a horizontal racket, but the concept remains. Bend your knees, take your waist down, keep your wrist low . . . see Illus. 17 again.

Half Volley Spin

The half volley is not an underspin shot. Even if you slice all your other strokes (volleys and groundstrokes, backhand and forehand alike), never cut down at a half volley—because then the direction of your racket head totally opposes the swiftly rising ball and invites a mis-hit.

It's far more sound for the racket to rise with the ball; and rising with the ball gives natural topspin. While you're at it, make it a gathering, round-the-ball overspin, for a feeling of safety and confidence. Hitting around the ball wraps it up between your strings and your body so that it can't fly away somewhere too far to your off side, and out.

Topspin allows you net clearance and at the same time prevents the springing ball from springing out, no matter what spin your opponent's shot carries. If his shot is a devastating topspin dipper (against which you need maximum control) your topspin bites into his topspin and increases the effect of your own topspin. That's like sharpening a carving knife on a honing steel with downward strokes towards your body, when the blade bites into the steel.

Earlier, we spoke of playing a backhand slice against a high-bouncing topspin serve. But that was for ease of stroke-making, and not for producing the most effective spin. With a topspin half volley, stroke-ease and most effective spin are combined— the upward lift of your racket matches the upward movement of the swiftly rising ball, and topspin is what you need to arc the low ball up over the net and down again.

When your opponent's shot carries topspin, the ball rebounds higher from your racket face. How handy it is that this same spin increases the effectiveness of your own.

Let's Play a Point

Illus. 18 (on the next page) sets the scene.

Now comes the accomplished TV shot you've seen a dozen times or more. This is how you play it: Turning well sideways with strong right leg, and bent knee, and straight spine and back, go for the ball very close to the ground. With your weight going forward, gather the ball with outside overspin and play it safely and firmly all the way back to the deep backhand side, CD, and move in. Your weight and the ball's half-volleyed spring make the shot feel almost effortless.

It looks like good tennis and it is. You served a good ball and the advantage seemed to be yours. Then your opponent hit a solid topspin backhand and reversed the advantage. But you

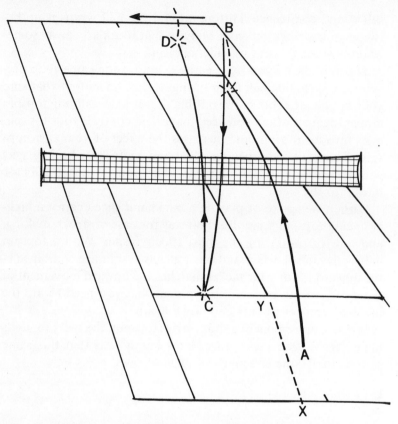

Illus. 18. EN-ROUTE BACKHAND HALF VOLLEY. AB is a fast twist serve and BC a strong topspin crosscourt backhand. The speed of the two shots hasn't given you time to be close enough to volley. You've moved in, X to about Y, and as your opponent finishes his backhand he moves towards the center of his baseline.

played an en route half volley with more ease and forward-moving balance than you would have gained from scraping a low backhand volley, almost making it seem that he had played into your hands. You've moved in and the advantage is now clearly yours.

It's Good for You

Good tennis from your opponent makes you play better—with a stronger outlook—knowing that only your best will do. It's more difficult when you begin a set against a player that you're told you'll beat comfortably if only you don't make too many mistakes. When this player makes a few unforced errors, you're likely to feel it would be a crime not to put every ball into play, and as a result you serve too softly and can easily degenerate into weakness on all your strokes. If you let that happen you find yourself constantly scrambling, with both your stroke-play and confidence at a low ebb. You probably manage to win, but you feel your game has gone back.

It's when your opponent plays good tennis and yet you feel your own game can beat it, that you play your best and feel like winning. So before a match starts don't fear that your opponent may play well today. Expect him to, and start strongly.

Grip

Use the Continental. You need flexibility and reach more than forward strength. Anyway, it's strong for hitting round the ball.

Half Volley in Front of Your Feet

Play it as a backhand if you can. This gives your racket some degree of slope away from the vertical and also allows your wrist to be free and out of line with your knees.

Caught in a fast forehand half volley in front of your toes near the net, you must use a vertical racket. Use a flat racket face and block the ball back over the net, using your fingers to absorb the speed of the ball.

You can't reduce the distance between your eye-level and the ball's level, either—because you can't bend your knees without bumping them into your racket, and bending your back only means over-balancing. All you can do is to watch the ball as well as possible, but it's essential to do that. *Drop your head distinctly down over the ball.* Anything else leaves your head too high up to see such a low ball clearly enough; you would be likely to mis-hit, and, even if it did hit the center of your strings, the ball would probably take a cue from your head and fly high.

It's not overly difficult to block an early-played ball over the net, with no backswing or timing to go wrong. Be a brick wall for a moment, but with eyes in your head and feel in your fingers.

SMASHING

Many smashes are overkilled or missed through attempted overkill. The two main requirements for winning points from smashing are to Be There and to time the ball well.

When you smash, your racket is *vertical*, and you hit in a vertical path for some distance. You also often hit fairly fast—and all this gives you a small margin for timing error. Be clear in your mind that for the stroke itself timing is just about everything.

Be There

No player gains a reputation for having a dangerous over-. head game merely because he resists the temptation to smash wildly or because he can deal solidly with short lobs well within his reach.

The player with the dangerous and solid overhead game is the one you simply can't get over, without lobbing the ball out.

Leaving position and anticipation aside, the first essential is to be able to move swiftly backwards while facing forwards and watching the ball, and to make a balanced spring. Illus. 19 shows a man doing this to the last ounce and inch.

While moving backwards keep your left hand forward. It provides good balance, and it will soon be needed again as an important part of your smashing action.

Generous Allowances

In a smash the ball is higher above the net than with any other stroke. Compared with a serve, you're closer to the net

Illus. 19. BE THERE. Play the ball back and move in again. The Continental grip gives you the greatest reach with racket face over ball.

and have the whole court to hit into—all this allows most generous net clearance. Stand at the net post one day when others are playing and surprise yourself about this net clearance.

Hit the ball downwards somewhere through this generous net clearance, but *always over* the net. Don't add to bad smashing statistics, which reveal that about 70 per cent of missed over-heads are down into the net.

You don't need to be able to smash everywhere, all over the court with angle or depth to either side. A solid smash deep to your opponent's backhand normally prevents him from doing anything else but toss again. So, if your present smashing is erratic build your overhead game on that shot alone while you gain confidence from success.

Don't think your need for depth is precise and cancels the luxury of your net clearance, because depth for smashing is also generous. A volley, to be effectively deep, may need to land inside the baseline by a yard or less, but a smash's awkward bounce makes two yards or more a deep shot. The baseline is the only boundary because the sidelines don't come into it.

The baseline is a friendly boundary to a smash, because a smash has a greater downward tendency than any other shot. If you hit with the center of your strings the ball will either land in court or go into the net. It never goes out from speed alone (good players demonstrate this with their successful speed) and it would be unnatural for you to aim higher than the top of the high net clearance available.

See Illus. 2 again. Your smash goes out only when you hit below center. What really happens is that your racket face is still tilted slightly backwards and hasn't come over the ball and hit the center—but you feel a below-center contact.

Always feel that a lob is coming somewhat towards you, as indeed it is, and not that it is dropping down on you like a ton of bricks. Then hit forward and down, and clear the net and land the ball inside the baseline.

If you let a skyscraping lob bounce fairly well back in court, play a half smash deep to your opponent's backhand, keeping in good balance so that you follow it in as an approach shot.

Timing and Action

Since timing is vital, it follows that your smash should involve the least action possible, while giving plenty of power. Until about the mid-1960s it was always decreed that your smashing action should be identical with your service. It should *not* be identical. To serve, take your racket up behind your back; to smash, take it up in front of your body.

To smash a ball moving towards you does not require all the wind-up and long-swinging service action that generates speed from a stationary ball propelled all the way from the baseline. You need no more action than that portrayed and described in Illus. 20.

Feel completely uncluttered, and concentrate on your timing.

Illus. 20. COMPACT, AND POWER TO BURN. Settling under the lob, put your left hand up to sight the ball (you can even use it for covering the sun), to balance yourself, and to prevent any right-side collapse. Take your racket up by the shortest route (in front of your body, not around behind it as in serving) and hold it ready near your right shoulder. Rise to meet the ball as necessary. (If it suits your game, come well in under the ball and rise to meet it whenever you can, as this gives you more positive timing, higher net clearance and freer movement.) Smash forward and downward, from the center of your strings, OVER the net.

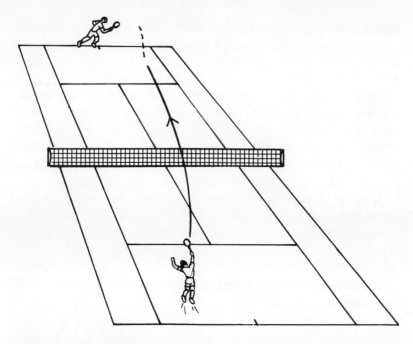

Illus. 21. FADING BACK TO SMASH A DEEP LOB TO YOUR BACKHAND SIDE. Make a forehand smash of it even if the ball's above your left shoulder. Rise to meet the ball so you won't be farther back than necessary. Have your racket face square to the ball to avoid a mis-hit, and from deep in court hit more forward than down.

Using Your Solid Overhead

Don't waste it by thinking that the first lob you receive necessarily has to be despatched in one blow. Every serve doesn't have to be an ace or you'd have faults galore. Give your overhead an even break.

While you're smashing you're winning. Sustained lobbing can't beat solid smashing, any more than a balloon can withstand an airgun.

When the first lob you receive is a good one (whether you forced a lob or your opponent chose to play one), play it firmly back to the deep backhand side, so that your opponent will lob again, and move in. If his second lob is even better than the first, fade back and play as shown in Illus. 21, and then move in again. He can't escape. He'll make a poor lob before you'll miss a firm smash.

It's no argument to say that there's more chance of missing during your sequence of smashes than if you'd tried to make a winner of the first one. You may as well say you should hit your first volley for a winner to avoid the possibilities of missing later ones or of being passed. Keep to solid first volleys and a solid carefully-timed overhead.

Despatch the first short lob you get, though. Never smash cautiously from so close to the net that your opponent's next lob sails over your head for a mortifying winner.

4. ALL-COURT GAME

The all-court game is a net-seeking game. You may think of yourself as an all-court player because you volley well, but you're not *playing* this game if you surrender the net almost completely to a net-game player. The same holds true if, against a baseliner, you confine your net play to waiting for a short slow ball to play to his backhand and follow in. In both examples you're playing virtually as a baseliner.

An all-court player's firm intention is to win from the net—the easier position—and if you're to play this game you must take the net whenever you can cover it.

You may play an all-court game for a number of reasons. You may normally be a net-game player but your service is temporarily tamed by the slow court surface, or you may always play all-court tennis because your serve (certainly your second ball) is not good enough for you to play a net game. Or you may play it because you volley long groundstrokes well but can't cope with first-volley court coverage against fast service returns. Or because you like the all-court game's tempo and tactics and choose to play it.

Whatever your reason, use every stroke and occasion to take the net—or probably you won't be playing it at all.

NET-SEEKING OPPORTUNITIES

Service

Depending upon how good your serve is, go in on all first serves, or on all first serves to the backhand, or on all first serves to the backhand in the left court that will land deep in the corner or awkwardly wide. Even if your opponent's backhand is his steadier shot, you're more likely to receive an easier first volley from it than from his forehand. Attack the forehand only if it is a weaker and slower shot with less topspin dip than the backhand, or if your opponent plays it wildly against fast first serves.

It may suit your game better to stay back and to follow in from a short return, which your first ball often brings. You're not confined to this though; you would like to be able to follow a first serve in whenever you want to, such as at game point—but more often than not you miss the very serve you want to follow in.

The cause is excitement and hurry; the result is right-side collapse. You may throw the ball up well, but before you hit it everything else happens first. You cut your left hand away too early, away from your body and down by your left side. This drops your left shoulder (and probably your head too, so that momentarily you don't see the ball properly) and this brings the whole of your right side and your swinging right leg over the baseline. All this happens *before* you've hit the ball. Down into the net it goes, and another opportunity for net play goes with it.

Using whichever concept suits you better, keep your right side back or your left side forward until you're striking the ball. To help keep your right (hitting) shoulder back, keep your right toe on the ground. To help keep your left side forward, either hold your left hand up longer or drop it in front of your body (instead of letting it swing wide) and serve across it. (See Illus. 9 again.) Many players use this crossed-arms follow-through, some unknowingly, some intentionally.

Keeping your back toe on the ground provides a steady platform but slightly slows your net advance. Obviously it's not suitable if you make your serve with a jumping action.

Deep Ground Strokes

Depth is the acknowledged basis of an all-court player's attack, but look for all extra chances to use it.

Examples: Your opponent returns a ball of yours that was not deep, but he tarries for a second instead of at once getting

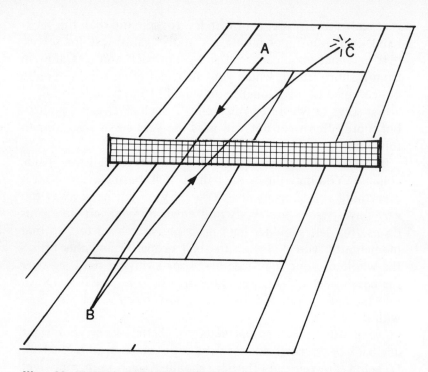

Illus. 22. IF YOUR OPPONENT TARRIES. Even though he has played AB fairly deep, if you take the ball early and play it to C (behind him) you can go into the net despite the length of the journey.

back behind his baseline. Play the ball early, and hit it behind him, and move in. (See Illus. 22.)

Or, you're hitting downwind (wind behind you) and you play a topspin drive high over the net (five feet or so) but you know from the feel of the ball on your strings that it will land just in. Your opponent prepares to play it from well back. All that distance, against the wind? Go in.

Short Balls

An old adage is never to come in on a short ball, but don't let that stop you.

Example: You drive deep to the forehand corner, your opponent makes a nondescript return and you play a backhand slice across to his backhand side. Your shot isn't fast or acutely angled, nor is it a drop-shot. It's a short ball that's a long way from your opponent and it's going to bounce low. He'll have to retrieve it, dig it up. Go in.

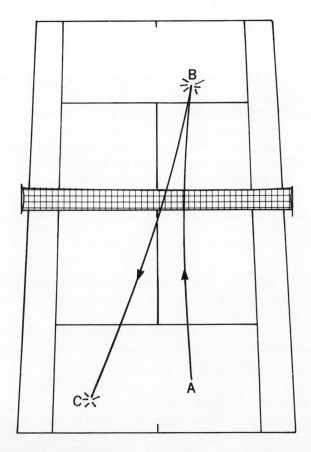

Illus. 23. UNEXPECTED ATTACK. Your BC is a fairly long half volley, but it turns defense into attack.

Half Volleys

A half volley that's been forced on you doesn't seem a likely shot to follow in, but it can be.

Example: A shortish ball brings you inside the baseline, but your reply is not good enough to follow in—and then your opponent's next shot apparently catches you at your feet. Rather than retreat and play a leaning-back groundstroke, look for the chance to send your weight forward and play a "half drive" type of backhand half volley, and move in. You haven't far to go. (See Illus. 23 on previous page.)

Lobs

When you lob over your opponent and he has to chase it, go in.

When he drives so fast and deep to your forehand corner that you have to hoist a high lob, it seems that the initiative remains with him. But if he has stayed back and your lob is going to land near the baseline and far enough on his backhand side to prevent him from moving around it and playing a half smash, the advantage is yours. He can't develop much power from his backhand in that position, so go in. The high lob gives you time.

Slider Forehand

A slider forehand is a shot you play with inside-underspin, curving the ball away to your off side and wide of your opponent's backhand. Its bounce goes away too and keeps lower than a flat ball. When a crosswind assists further, you can make a penetrating approach shot of it instead of merely rallying the ball over and staying back. (See Illus. 24.)

NOTE: Use any crosswind to attack in the direction of the wind with controlled shots and follow in, making your opponent play at full stretch—after which he has to hit back against the crosswind. When hitting yourself out of trouble or defending, hit into the crosswind and use it as a cushion.

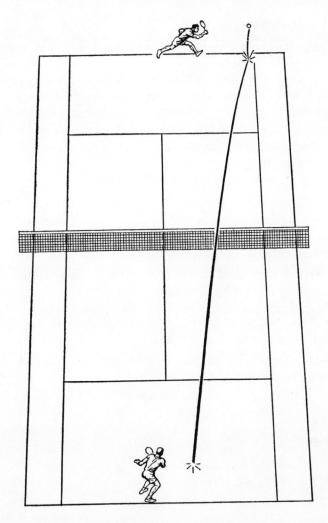

Illus. 24. SLIDER FOREHAND. All this swerve and a crosswind too.

Chip-Approach Shot

This is your all-court stock-in-trade—a cut or fairly short slice played on the move and followed to the net. An easily-made stroke, it allows you to concentrate on control.

Place it exactly. Use the exact speed needed to allow you to reach your best net position before your opponent hits the ball, forcing him to attempt his passing shot against a poised net man instead of a hurried new arrival. Its bounce is low, reducing his passing angle.

Develop a range of chip-approach shots:

● With balls above shoulder height, chip outside and down.

● With forehands below net height and going to your opponent's backhand, slide your racket inside and under—and to his forehand chip outside and under.

● With low backhand across to backhand, chip outside and under—and to the forehand, slide your racket inside and under.

Because most chip shots are played from net height or lower and to a right-hander's backhand, most players fully develop only the forehand inside-and-under shot and the backhand outside-and-under. It's another reason why you may be less effective against a left-hander.

When playing approach shots keep your mind thinking forward, or you'll never glide to the net without hurry. Body too, so that your weight moves you in and keeps the ball firmly down.

An onlooker sees your playing an approach shot and moving to the net as being one fluid motion, but always make at least a mental pause between the two. Set yourself up and hit firmly with long contact towards your chosen spot—and then close in.

If you hurry to get to the net you'll rush your approach shot, and this may result in two common errors. The first is that you meet the ball somewhat farther in front of your body than intended and in the upward part of your swing, and then you have to slow your shot down or it will go out. It causes you to play a milder approach shot than you mean to.

On the forehand side, the second common error of haste is that your right side swings around too soon. It's hardly a right-side collapse, but it spoils your shot for pace and direction.

If you don't realize that your approach shots are not as good as they should be, you credit your opponent with having better passing shots than he really has. You tend to hang back, forgoing all-court opportunities.

Center Theory

The Center Theory is an invaluable tactic in using your chip-approach shot. If you play your approach shot deep down the center, particularly with a low bounce, and follow in, you restrict the angles open to your opponent. It's the *center* ball, not the wider one (if he can get behind it), that leaves him the least room for a passing shot. Playing the Center Theory you can expect to make a first volley from your approach shot, just as a net-game player expects to make a first volley from his serve.

There are many occasions where an approach shot to either corner would not prevent your opponent from getting behind the ball and passing you on either side; so you would have to remain on your baseline. Played as Center-Theory approach shots, however, they provide constant net-seeking opportunities that would otherwise be lost.

YOUR OPPONENT'S GAME

So far—through net-game until now—you've mostly been playing your own game; only the Anticipation discussion has served notice that your opponent's game demands recognition. This demand increases in all-court tennis, where your net attacks are greatly influenced by your opponent's game.

Your own game always matters most, but if you don't count your opponent's as well, you don't "know the game." It's not enough merely to notice that your opponent is left-handed or two-handed or that he cuts his groundstrokes. That's saying single-handed right-handers with a forehand drive are all alike, except for their general standard of play. You'll lose more than net opportunities that way—you can lose the whole match by not realizing the extent of an unknown opponent's strength or by not fully exploiting a weakness he may have covered up.

In contrast, if you recognize his game, no opponent remains a stranger; he at once becomes a type of player you've played before.

Be clear about that. Some self-taught players may believe that their own games must be unique, because they (no one else) taught themselves to play; and some players who pride themselves on their individualism may imagine that their tennis style is correspondingly individualistic. But in fact they all hold their rackets with a grip akin to one or another of the grips all players use. The grip influences the style, and the style (which is what you see) in turn produces remarkably similar strengths and weaknesses.

Older players recognize new opponents' games from years of experience. Others may do so in a short time by having a sharp eye for a weakness.

Probably the best method of sizing up your opponents is through an understanding of grips and styles. With a thorough grasp of that picture you can know your opponent's game as early as during the warm-up. You can't help seeing a player's style, even though you're watching the ball yourself.

Extreme styles, at least, and their inherent weaknesses are associated in most players' minds. When you tell an enquirer, "He was Western—I kept out of his reach all right," you've told him everything.

If you can immediately notice the difference between Continental- and Western-grip players, it takes only a little finer tuning to recognize the grips and styles in between, namely, Australian, Eastern, Extreme-Eastern, and Semi-Western.

Taking different types of left-handers and two-handers, etc. into account seems to make quite a list—but it's finite. Short, too, in comparison with all the players you'll meet in the future.

PLAYING VARIOUS BASELINE STYLISTS

(Detailed descriptions of Grips and Styles are in Appendix 1.)
Unorthodox or unusual styles show the greatest difference
between strengths and weaknesses.

WESTERN-STYLE PLAYERS

A Western-grip player likes to meet the ball well in front of
his body and when it's bouncing high. Here he produces the
strongest and most difficult passing shots of any type of player.
He doesn't like low or wide balls on either forehand or backhand
and abhors all those that get behind him.

So, against a Western-grip player, play wide and then put the
ball behind him and follow in. It is usually safer to play your
first shot to his backhand. From there he is less likely to spoil
your plan by making a strong shot and taking charge of the
rally himself. You will then be taking the net against his strong
forehand, but if you've placed the ball behind him it won't
matter.

Western Forehand Only

If your opponent has a Western forehand only and hits his
backhand in the normal way with the opposite face of the
racket, it means that he has to make the largest change of grip
imaginable to reach an adequate backhand grip. Few Western
forehand-only players change grip as much as that, and in consequence have an inadequate backhand grip and a physically
weak stroke. So now you have two points for attack: the weaker
than normal backhand (from lack of leverage) and the stronger
than normal forehand (which you beat by putting the ball
behind your opponent).

Two-Handed Western

A Western forehand-only player may use a two-handed
backhand, in which he doesn't change his right-handed forehand grip but merely adds the left hand and hooks his backhand

strongly over the net. At first thought he seems to have solved his difficulties. He has a Continental player's advantages of not having to change grip and of having a good balance between forehand and backhand strength; and at the same time he has a physically stronger forehand and backhand than the Continental player.

There are large flaws in this style of course, or it would have been adopted years ago and perhaps have driven out all others. Its Western forehand remains restricted in reaching wide balls and is clumsy both in handling low balls and balls behind the player. The two-handed backhand can hook balls behind it well enough, but using two hands restricts a wide reach. So the player is restricted in reach on both sides.

Semi-Western

The forehand of a Semi-Western player has a similar looped appearance to the Western. Awkwardness against balls that are low, wide or behind the player remain its greatest weakness, even though it is made from a less Westerly grip.

The Semi-Western forehand grip is the same as the Extreme-Eastern forehand grip, though its looped-topspin style is different. Backhand variations are the same as those of the Extreme-Eastern style—discussed next.

EXTREME-EASTERN STYLE

The forehand looks like a powerful Eastern, with a preference for shoulder-high instead of waist-high balls.

The grip, about halfway between Eastern and Western, is the same as the Semi-Western. But the Extreme-Eastern player's forehand is a forward-topspin stroke (in fact and in looks) and not a looped-topspin one. His reach is better, because the EE player does not meet the ball as far in front of his body as the Semi-Western player.

This powerful forehand is the EE player's point-winner and you need to keep clear of it. That's not easy to do if he's one of those EE players who steps around his backhand and plays his forehand from anywhere to everywhere.

Backhand

An EE player's backhand can be Western, which means that he plays the ball with the same face of the racket as that used for the forehand. What you see him do is turn his racket head in a semi-circle over his wrist and play the ball *well* ahead of his body. You can't mistake it—and then you know at once that he has poor reach on that side. All you need to observe next is whether his backhand is a sweeping topspin drive or whether he relies on a solid but defensive push or prod with a flat racket face and you know what to expect of his backhand side.

Or, if you see your EE opponent playing a normal-looking backhand, then the main thing is to see whether it's rolled or sliced.

Less obvious, but still easy to see is that in order to play this normal-looking backhand he must make a large change of grip. He must do so, because it's a long way around the handle from an EE forehand grip to an Adequate backhand grip. (See Illus. 25 on next page.)

This large change of grip takes time. Play your approach shots to the backhand fast and fairly close to the body and make your opponent attempt his passing shots with only a makeshift grip.

To avoid this large change of grip your EE opponent may have an Inadequate backhand grip, as shown in Illus. 26.

If your opponent has neither the strong backhand shown in Illus. 25 nor the weak stroke shown in Illus. 26, he'll probably have a modest in-between type of backhand made by using the Australian forehand grip as his backhand grip. (Get your racket out and try it for yourself: take an Australian forehand grip on your racket and use it for a neatly-made backhand with your wrist held well back so that the racket head can come

Illus. 25. ADEQUATE BACKHAND GRIP. "Adequate" is a handy collective term for Continental and Eastern backhand grips (for their differences, and for past confusions, see Appendix 1). The term "Adequate" describes the normal backhand grip—which is neither weakly inadequate nor over-strongly stiff, and not Western either.

Illus. 26. INADEQUATE BACKHAND GRIP. The weakest grip and most obviously "Inadequate" is the Eastern forehand grip for the backhand, because you play with the wrist bent and the back of the hand facing forward. (Shown here.) The best "Inadequate" grip is the Australian forehand grip, played with the wrist held low and back so that the racket face comes outside the ball. Sound enough for a low volley, this still doesn't produce strong passing shots from the back of the court.

firmly around and outside the imaginary ball. You will see that you have to play the ball well back beside your body, and preferably from fairly low down after letting it drop.) The strength of this type of backhand doesn't compare with an EE player's strong topspin forehand, played from ahead of his body and at the top of the bounce.

If an EE player has lop-sided strength he always plays rallies standing to the left of center of his baseline, to give full rein to his forehand. When he steps round his backhand he hits hard, in either direction, to compensate for his bad court position. When you try to play your approach shots so close to his backhand sideline that he can't possibly run round the ball, you often overdo things and hit over the sideline instead of just inside it. It's better to hit to his forehand side first and then play your approach shot to his opened backhand side, but you have to be sure that your first shot doesn't allow his forehand point-winner to take charge at once. Keep the bounce of your shot as low as possible.

Then, when you do play your approach shot to his opened backhand, make sure you mentally set yourself up and hit firmly towards your chosen spot—then close in. If he is able to step around any milder approach shot than you meant, he will extract full toll.

LEFT-HANDERS

Most players don't like playing against left-handers, if only because the ball comes from a different direction. All-court players don't like a left-hander's backhand being on the wrong side, reducing the effectiveness of their own attack. Worst of all, some left-handers play angles that seem to be all their own.

Warming-up against a left-hander, the main thing to learn is not his grip and style but his *type*. His type determines his game.

Balanced Left-Handers

Some left-handers play the normal game of right-handers; the forehand is the stronger side and is played with some degree of roll or topspin, and the backhand, probably the steadier side, is played with a little underspin. This type of play does not give rise to abnormal angles.

The real difference here is that a left-hander's wrong-side backhand reduces the effectiveness of your own more usual stroking, namely, your down-the-line forehand, crosscourt backhand, inside-underspin forehand chip approach, and your outside-underspin backhand chip approach. A left-hander has a natural advantage, but at least the remedy—widening your stroke-range—is in your own hands.

Meanwhile, you have a couple of compensating factors. First, you serve well to a left-hander in the right court, even your second serve easily finding his backhand. Second, if his balance in strength comes from having a solid two-handed backhand he often has to cover its lack of reach by exposing his forehand side, to which you can play the shots you're used to directing to a right-hander's backhand. Keep your going-away slider forehand well in mind.

Backhanded Left-Hander

Some left-handers feel stronger and more natural with their left side forward, and the backhand is their strength. You can see it clearly, from their whole approach to the ball, from their swift and natural footwork and from the confident backhand stroke they make. Obviously, they are right-handed swingers with a baseball or cricket bat.

The forehand is an inconspicuous sort of shot, many of these players only cutting it. It is more open to your attack than any right-hander's backhand is, because no one can step around a ball and use his backhand with anything like the speed and effectiveness of running round a backhand and using a forehand. To this extent, any weak forehand is worse than a weak backhand, and if it's a weak left-handed forehand it is open to your usual-direction attack as well.

Forehand-Strength Left-Hander

Most left-handers are specialists on the forehand, and on the backhand many are virtually make-do's. This stems from their left-court doubles play of earlier years. The left-handers who play angles "all their own" are in this class.

The master shot is a forehand topspin crosscourt drive—made with a fairly long swing and nearly always Eastern or Extreme Eastern in style. The left-hander hits:

- Crosscourt to the deep backhand corner
- Crosscourt near the service line and across to the side fence
- Crosscourt and dipping into your backhand half volley

as you approach

• Crosscourt slowly and accurately right across your body when you're at the net.

If you overprotect against this last shot, the left-hander does not change to a flatter or inside-spin forehand (a telegram you could detect) but "crosscourts down-the-line" somewhat in the manner of Shot B in Illus. 7. As a forehand specialist, he does it from a ball either inside or outside his sideline.

You understand him, but his direction remains hard to anticipate and his angles within his crosscourt directions are all his own. But you must look at that the other way around: that his angles may be all his own, but at least you know him.

These long-swinging forehand specialists don't like changing grip for the backhand. Particularly those playing a punishing Extreme-Eastern style forehand have only an Inadequate backhand grip and most, EE and Eastern alike, tend to play the backhand shot with raised elbow and dropped racket head and resultant inside-underspin.

Clearly, then, this indifferent backhand is the target for your attack, but, like right-handed EE players of unbalanced strength between forehand and backhand, a forehand-strength left-hander is adept at running around his backhand whenever possible, making it difficult to find. Once found, however, a left-hander's inside-underspin backhand is much better played to his off side, down the line; as a crosscourt passing shot it's often the weakest shot on the court.

When you move in after a good approach shot to the backhand—alert to cover either a down-the-line shot or an attempted lob over your backhand side, and at the same time feeling confident that your opponent's crosscourt backhand is not dangerous—then suddenly the powerful forehand-strength left-hander becomes more like Samson without his hair.

Strong-Forehand Left-Hander Yourself

For your net-approach attack, your stroke preferences of crosscourt forehand and down-the-line backhand go naturally to a right-hander's backhand. At the net, your opponent's favored passing shots go to your wider and stronger forehand volley.

You well know that mere left-handedness doesn't make you an unbeatable all-court player. But with the same skills—stroke ability, reflexes, position or whatever—you're harder to beat than if you were right-handed. Know that it's always your opponent who carries the extra weight.

PLAYING ANOTHER LEFT-HANDER. If he's the same strong-forehand type that you are, his preferred shots go towards your forehand strength and he doesn't like playing you any more than you like playing him. Make sure you get a good net position against his backhand more often than he does against yours.

If he's a balanced left-hander he's still a left-hander and his stroke preference is towards your forehand, the strongest shot on the court. You can regard him almost as a right-hander. Unless he's a player who can attack your vulnerable backhand well, he dislikes playing you more than you mind his type of left-handed game.

If he's a backhanded left-hander, his weak forehand is in for the pasting of its life.

CUT PLAYERS

They're an all-court player's dream. If you keep the bounce of your approach shot below net height there's little safe angle open for crosscourt passing shots, and a cut ball rises fairly straight and is easy to volley.

Against your net position his most likely replies are down the line or a lob over your backhand side.

BIG BACKHAND OPPONENT

This type, by all appearances once a left-hand swinger, is clearly strongest with his right side forward. He has a very fast topspin backhand, strongly made with his thumb straight up the back of the handle. Even if you can't see that, you can certainly see him meeting the ball far in front of his body. His forehand side is only a small cut, mainly underspin, usually made with an Australian or Eastern grip.

He likes playing against erratic baseliners, where his safe small cut seldom misses and his big backhand hits winners.

You mainly approach against his cut, which is easy to volley and particularly unsuitable for him to play crosscourt with any speed if it is to remain in court. If you get the ball well behind his backhand, his big shot can only punish the side fence.

CHOPPED FOREHAND

This player is much better balanced. His forehand chop is a strong and fairly long downward stroke made with a Continental grip. (You may not see his grip, but if you were chopping strongly downward yourself you'd grip your racket that way.) His shot carries a lot of outside spin; it skids low on a fast surface and clogs low on a soft one. Here's a shot in which the bounce is a noteworthy part of it; the usual purpose of spin is mainly to control the ball's flight.

When made from a high-bouncing ball this man's chop curves away from your forehand, perhaps right out of reach. (See Illus. 27.)

He has a strong backhand—rolled, since most good players have a rolled shot on at least one side. With shots like these, he's a purposeful player, used to winning his matches. In the warm-up you can see his groundstroke game will be too strong for yours if you remain at the baseline. So despite his rolled backhand and the wide forehand reach his Continental-grip chop gives him, for you it has to be net or nothing.

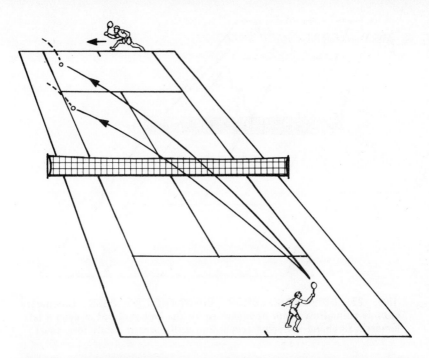

Illus. 27. DOWNWARD CHOP. Your opponent's outside spin makes the ball curve and bounce right away from you—if you are back at your baseline. On a hard high-bouncing court, this type of player is severe on retriever-only players. He'd prefer you not to be an all-court player.

In taking the net against his backhand get the ball somewhat behind him, to lessen the weight and dip of his rolled shot. Avoid playing high-bouncing balls to his forehand chop. (See Illus. 28 on next page.)

The basis of your net-approach tactics is to try to reduce his downward outside-spin chop to an inside-underspin cut, so play your chip-approach shots with low bounce. With a ball well below net height there's not much room above the ground for him to make his downward outside-spin chop, even though he determinedly tries by bouncing his racket frame down into

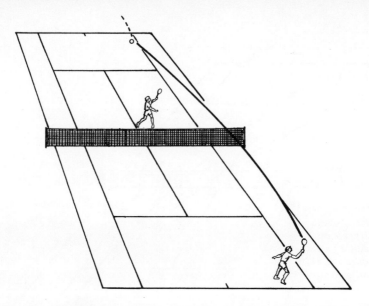

Illus. 28. DOWNWARD CHOP, DOWN-THE-LINE PASS. Downward outside spin allows your opponent to hit the ball well out of even a left-hander's forehand volleying reach, and still curve it safely into court.

the court. Mostly, your trapped opponent's shot turns from outside-spin to inside-underspin, and that's not good for a passing shot down the line. (See Illus. 29.) It's no use for crosscourt either, wide of your forehand volley, because the crosscourt direction of the ball overcomes any intended in-curve and the ball flies straight—straight over the sideline too, unless played with gentle touch.

Confined to using inside-underspin, your opponent will probably choose to play a mixture of down-the-line touch shots (to make you play backhand half volleys) and tosses over your backhand side (if he's able to draw you in too far in trying to avoid them). It's a much milder game than he intended playing.

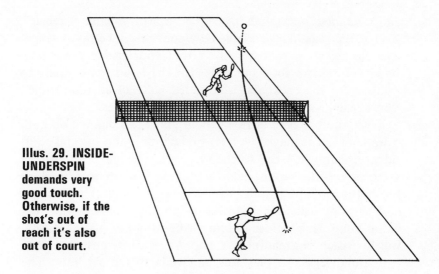

Illus. 29. INSIDE-UNDERSPIN demands very good touch. Otherwise, if the shot's out of reach it's also out of court.

TWO-HANDED

A double-hander used to be classed as a freak stroke and was always its user's outstanding shot. But it has grown into wide use and may merely be a means of strengthening an otherwise weak backhand.

The normal two-handed player is a right-hander with a two-handed backhand. If his two-hander is a swinging rolled stroke it is probably his stronger side. If it's a short and solid block, the forehand is the point winner. Lack of reach is the inherent weakness of every type of two-handed player.

If a left-hander uses a two-handed backhand it is almost certainly for backhand solidity. But make sure at once that he *is* left-handed; if he hasn't already shown you a practice serve, send up a lob. If he serves or smashes right-handed without any awkwardness, he's a right-hander with a two-handed *forehand*. Looking at him with new eyes you can see he's put all his eggs in one basket—his left-handed forehand is the weakest shot on the court and invites your attack.

If your opponent has a two-handed forehand but uses a

single-handed backhand instead of a wrong-hand forehand, his backhand is likely to have very poor reach, certainly whenever he has to play it quickly. (Hold your racket for a two-handed forehand shot and note that the hand that's going to be used for the backhand is stranded halfway up the handle.) Short reach is this player's trouble, on both sides.

If yet another type of two-hander plays two-handed on both sides, one side is played with crossed hands and is his makeshift side. Probably it's the forehand, the stroke he plays on the same side as his serving hand—because his serving hand, at the bottom of the handle, would be in the way. However on *both* sides he usually has stronger-than-normal shots when the ball is comfortably close to him, or he wouldn't play that way. But his reach is dreadful (the poorest reach of any man with two sound legs); so play low and wide to the sidelines. The crosshands forehand has the shortest reach of any stroke you're ever likely to see.

There's a great difference in viewing each type of two-hander through his weakness instead of being befuddled by his unorthodoxy.

AGAINST MORE USUAL BASELINE STYLES

Your usual opponents are right-handed and single-handed, playing in the Continental, Australian or Eastern styles. Of these, the Continental players are fewest in number.

CONTINENTAL STYLE (See Appendix 1)

You can recognize a Continental player by seeing him take the ball farther back beside his body than other players do, and by his low wrist on forehand and backhand. Both characteristics are caused by his grip. He shows complete naturalness between forehand and backhand (because he uses the same grip for both, except that perhaps he advances his thumb diagonally across the handle for the backhand).

Properly played by an accomplished player, the Continental style offers no inherent weakness to your all-court game's net attack. The forehand gives the best flexibility of any style in dealing with balls that are low, wide, or behind the player, and it has no weakness against a medium net-high ball. If you play high over the net for a high bounce, the Continental player can either take the ball on the rise or else let it bounce high and play a long and downward outside-spin slice or chop, for which his grip is ideally suited. And in any case you can't base your net-approach on high-bouncing balls. On the backhand, his no-change grip gives him time to play a rolled stroke as his basic shot.

Actually it's different. For example, your opponent is quite likely to undercut his backhand, giving you an attacking point for your low-bouncing chip-approach.

However, it's his forehand you scrutinize. To play it properly a Continental player needs to roll his wrist early in his forward swing so that the racket face is square to the ball for a reasonable time before hitting it. This gives him a sound stroke, either flat or rolled, made with easy timing. A Continental player needs to know this, and he needs to have a strong enough wrist to do it.

Stiff-Wristed Forehand

As often as not (more often than not with lesser players) the player does not roll his wrist and close his racket face, but finds it much easier to play with his wrist held rather stiffly for strength. This causes his forward swing to the ball to be made with his racket face slightly open, tilted upwards. For a player basing his forehand on roll, his timing becomes demanding, and when he wants to hit the ball flat intentionally his timing has to be almost exact. It's an unsound forehand, and for safety has to be played carefully rather than fast. Try this in slow motion with your racket.

Many stiff-wristed Continental players find a "flat" forehand drive easier to make than a rolled one. They imagine their shot to be flat but it isn't, the open-faced racket giving a slight slice to the ball. Aimed crosscourt this slice has backspin; aimed to the off side it has inside-underspin; but the point is that it always has a little underspin. Underspin holds the ball up and makes it easy to volley, and it also makes your opponent's crosscourt passing shot likely to miss the sideline.

Stiff-wristed forehand players have a better backhand than forehand. This backhand is not obtrusively strong like a Big Backhand, so you may not notice that it is really the stronger side—when all the time the forehand should have been the main target for your net attack.

You will easily notice a stiff-wristed forehand.

Erratic Forehand

Seen more easily from the side than the front, there's a serious flaw in the forehand technique of some free-wristed Continental players. Although the wrist is free it isn't rolled over to close the racket face early in the forward swing; the face is left open until just before contact and then whipped over into position.

The shot is fast and the momentum of the whipping-over racket face produces topspin; but because of the over-demanding timing it requires it must be erratic. It can't stand up to pressure and it breaks down many times against easy balls on vital points. It provides probably the best example of a good-looking strokemaker being thought wrongly to have poor match temperament.

If this shot's yours, you know the remedy. If it's your opponent's . . . well, you're on the court to win.

AUSTRALIAN STYLE (See Appendix 1)

Like the well-played Continental style, the well-played Australian style offers no weaknesses to your all-court net attack. The practical difference between the two is that the Australian style is easier to play well. The forehand grip has the palm only *towards* the top surface of the handle, instead of being above it and so there is less demand for a strong wrist and less likelihood of developing Continental forehand flaws. With no more than a small change of grip for the backhand there's time for a rolled stroke.

It's perhaps interesting to note that the Australian style which had no name until recently and had to be described as being somewhere between Continental and Eastern, is now so widely used throughout the world that all one can say about recognizing it is that it looks normal. It would only be going backward to say that it looks about halfway between the more distinctive Continental and Eastern.

For what it's worth: the forehand plays the ball from about opposite the left heel and the backhand from ahead of the right foot, and the forehand is usually the stronger side. It has more forward power than the Continental, less than the sweeping Eastern. It looks less low-wristed than the Continental but does not drop the racket head to a low ball as the Eastern often does.

Although there are no inherent weaknesses in the style itself, that doesn't apply to its users and you have to find their individual weaknesses. For example, many Australian-style players slice their backhands. They began to do so for safety, while they attacked with their forehands, and the shot became their only backhand. When they need to play a passing shot from a low ball they can't produce a more damaging topspinner.

EASTERN (See Appendix 1)

The Eastern forehand grip places the racket handle more in line with the forearm (when viewed from the front) than the Continental or Australian. To you at the other end of court it looks long-armed with the player sweeping the ball strongly with his weight well behind it. With drives below thigh height the racket head looks a little dropped.

Wide balls are effectively played because a sweeping stroke is at its best when the ball is wide and the player moves across to it. Balls behind the player put him in difficulty and those only fairly close to his body cramp him somewhat.

The grip-change for an Adequate backhand is fairly large. Some players change a full quarter of a circle to make a long topspin drive similar to their forehands—and these players' bodies are the target for your approach shots. Others, who concentrate on forehand strength, make less change and sometimes play with only a small cut as their backhand.

In fast play on fast surfaces the grip-change is the Eastern style's weakness—and the reason for the Australian forehand grip becoming popular.

AGAINST ALL OPPOSING BASELINE STYLES

Your viewpoint as a net-seeking all-court player is that there is no opposing style or type of player incapable of being attacked, only that some are more easily attacked than others. Note that the less orthodox styles develop a strength but breed a weakness, and are the easiest to attack. A completely orthodox style is not invulnerable—its weakness may be overall mildness, with no strength anywhere to hurt you.

Play the warm-up to get warm and to get your feet moving quickly and strongly and your shots in their groove—and to know your opponent. Never be a detective peering for clues. But be a tennis player knowing your opponent—if not by the end of the warm-up, fairly soon after.

A hard-to-beat opponent knows you.

NOTE: Playing groundstrokes is left to the next chapter, Baseline Game.

AGAINST ANOTHER ALL-COURT PLAYER

Don't be relegated to the role of baseliner. Let your opponent play that part.

If he'll have none of it, the game becomes a battle for the net. Be well aware that most opportunities for either of you will come from receiving a short ball. Try to play none, not even with your second serve, and you will probably get more than your share of the net.

AGAINST A NET-GAME PLAYER

Most of your opportunities to have the net will occur when you serve. But if you don't keep your mind on it, four or five games will slip by without your having played a single volley. Don't let any net-game player impose his tactics on you and deny you yours.

When You Serve

Part of your opponent's tactics is to take your second serve at the top of its bounce or earlier and play a chip-approach shot and follow in. Keep your second serve deep to prevent him from doing that and to force some amount of groundstroke rallying; then be determined that the first net sortie will be yours.

Don't squander any first serves. You'll get a lot into play if you serve either with the intention of following in or of preventing him from making an approach shot.

When Your Opponent Serves

On his service games don't be content with an unvarying pattern of his volleying and your playing an answering number of groundstrokes, even though you win some of the points. That's *his* pattern, a winning one. You can't break it if his serve continually puts you out of balance by being wide or jammed into your body. But nobody serves as well as that continually. On every one of his serves, first and second, move quickly and try to get behind the ball, so that you play either a dipping topspin drive or a short low block with your weight going forward in line with the ball. With this balance you can follow in if you see your shot is going perfectly and will give him a difficult volley.

If you follow in and play a winning volley from his defensive volley, or even a downward one, you get into a strong counter-attacking mood and you dent his morale as well.

To avoid this position he may try to _rush_ the net for his first volley, and this makes him easier to pass with your service return whether you're in balance or not. It also exposes him to a lob. The easiest and safest lobs to play are from your forehand in the right court over a right-handed net-rusher's backhand side and from your backhand in the left court over a left-hander's backhand. The main thing with either lob is to get it well out of reach, not just out of reach for a winner-in-one.

A net-game player usually has a better serve than you have (as an all-court player) and possibly is a better volleyer, as well. But you like to volley too, and must show him he doesn't own the net.

WHEN NOT TO APPROACH

Even though your opponent is back at his baseline (discounting whether he normally plays net game, all-court, or baseline tennis), there are some shots and positions that you can't approach from—some obvious, some not so. The following examples all assume him to be at the baseline and that the ball takes a normal bounce.

Short Balls

Don't follow in when your groundstroke lands shortish, either near the center of the court or near the sideline—in each case a ball he can get comfortably behind. You won't rattle him into making a mistake. From such a short range he'll pass you, on either side. Nothing builds a player's confidence more than hitting clean winners; don't present him with one.

Too Far Back

If your opponent plays deep and you return the ball from behind the baseline, don't expect to go up. It takes you too long to reach a good net position. En route you're too exposed

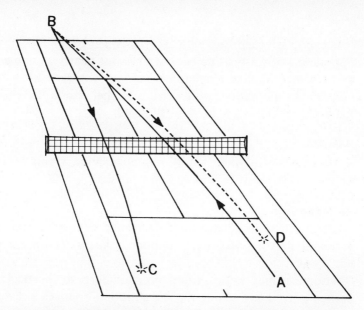

Illus. 30. DON'T APPROACH FROM A CROSSCOURT FOREHAND.
Although your crosscourt forehand AB is deep, you will not have time to
approach along a diagonal path and reach a good net-coverage position.
While approaching, your position is bad. You're wide open to his passing
shot BC. If you approached more diagonally to cover it, his crosscourt
BD would not even need to be angled sharply.

on either side, so you're not pressuring him with the need to
make a very strong shot. See Illus. 3 again; if you were back
near the service line, you'd have to reach wider to cover the
passing shots shown there.

Crosscourt

Similarly, you should not follow in on a forehand crosscourt
shot made from only fairly deep in your court. Your diagonal
path to a good net position takes you as much time to cover as
a straight one from behind your baseline, and your position is
worse. Your backhand side is wide open to your opponent's
down-the-line passing shot, and it is impossible to cover this
without exposing your forehand-volley side to an easily made
crosscourt. (See Illus. 30.)

It's not so clear-cut with a crosscourt backhand if your opponent's down-the-line backhand is not nearly as dangerous as his down-the-line forehand. Even so, you're a lot safer if your backhand shot is played from farther inside the baseline than your forehand is at A in Illus. 30.

Balance

Don't come in when you're out of balance, trying to make up time by rushing in. You're easily passed.

Trumped Ace

Don't refuse to believe the evidence of your own eyes when you find that an occasional opponent has a trump for your ace.

Your ace may be an approach shot deep to the backhand corner, played as a strong topspin shot that bounces awkwardly high. It's always been a great point-winner, forcing either weak attempts to pass you down the line or lobs within your reach, and it's a shot that you wouldn't like any opponent to play against you. It's your ace.

Suddenly you meet a player who likes it, who thrives on a deep high ball. He confidently plays a strong downward backhand slice against your topspin bounce, from the top of the bounce or slightly on the rise, and three times out of three he either passes you down the line or skims the ball low over the center-band and then wins with his next shot. See Illus. 28 and 27 again, imagining the shot to be a backhand and played from somewhat lower down.

Accept that your opponent has this particular shot in his locker, and don't keep playing your ace for him to trump. He makes capital out of your normally-awkward shot. Next time use a chip approach shot and keep the bounce low.

Rather than lose three points finding out, recognize this counterattack type of player from the way he handles the first situation. As you shape for your approach shot he tarries a little, drawing you into playing that deep-backhand-corner stroke—and next instant he's over behind it and playing his strong winner-in-one or winner-in-two. Probably you'd try a second time, being reluctant to forgo your proved point-winner after one setback, but don't take overlong to be convinced.

Down-the-Line Backhand Problems

If your backhand is your better side and you feel you can direct balls accurately with it, don't get carried away with your down-the-line performance or it may cost you more points than you win.

In each of the following examples imagine that you have played a deep crosscourt backhand and your opponent's return is shortish to your backhand—just where you want it, to make an approach shot from your better side. The average player would play to the backhand once more, but you're going to play a more penetrating shot down the line and follow in.

Example One. Your shot lands shorter than intended. (This can easily happen. Unlike playing a forehand away from your body, when you play a backhand to your off side you lose a little power—unknowingly, because you're concentrating too much on moving in without getting the stroke set first.) The ball is on your opponent's forehand and he comes diagonally across and *forward* to it, and with this momentum he can concentrate on control and pass you with certainty.

Example Two. A little later a similar situation occurs, and this time you determinedly play deep down the line with a steady slice to give you time to get into a net-covering position. But your shot is a shade too slow and your opponent gets behind it, eagerly behind it, and from there he can drive a strong passing shot on either side of you.

Example Three. This time his backhand return is a little wider and you again play down the line and follow in. You've played a strong shot—but that means that the ball will be back earlier, and in any case your wider starting point means you have farther to go to cover a possible crosscourt pass. You rush

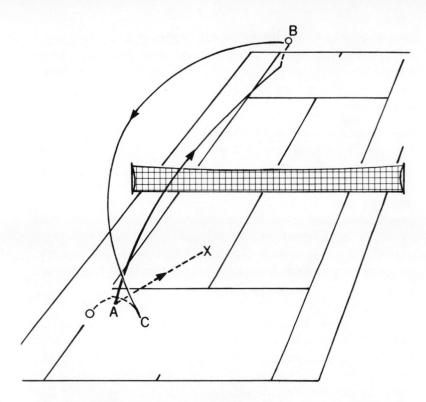

Illus. 31. DOWN-THE-LINE BACKHAND PITFALL. You've played a deep crosscourt backhand and your opponent has returned rather short and wide to your backhand (neither shot shown). You play AB as a fast approach shot and RUSH towards your net position at X. You rush under and away from BC, lobbed over your vacated backhand side. BC doesn't need to be much of a lob, either.

towards your net position—and when you rush you're always vulnerable to a good shot. In this example you rush under and away from a toss that sails over your vacated backhand side and beats you by miles. (See Illus. 31.)

Successful Down-the-Line Backhand Approach

When you're going down the line after first setting things up with your deep crosscourt, it's better to see your attack as a near-winner rather than as a normal approach shot. The wind can assist here. A crosswind blows the ball farther out of your opponent's forehand reach and a downwind may add enough speed to prevent his getting behind it.

If you're an accurate backhand player don't hold the defeatist belief that a windy day aids a robust player and always penalizes an accurate one.

Crosscourt Is Usually Sounder

The wind's not blowing. You play a deep crosscourt backhand, your opponent returns it shortish to your backhand and sets off to cover his open forehand sideline. Don't choose the non-percentage down-the-line approach shot. Play deep crosscourt again, or wide crosscourt, or down towards the center mark, straight at his moving body and if possible create a tangle of ball, racket, legs.

You've put the ball in his court, and you've got the net; he has no likely winner-in-one. Your play's as sound as a bell.

5. BASELINE GAME

If the baseline game is your most effective game, play it.

More players play it than any other game. Admittedly, some are forced to by lack of volleying ability or net coverage and some by a physical handicap in limb or eyesight, and some don't realize they've become relegated to the baseline. Even so, most players play a baseline game from choice, feeling more secure in their groundstrokes than in making net sorties.

The best baseliner is one who makes volleyers dive and scramble for the ball, not one who chases their neat placements. Defensive play, especially the retriever-only type, may beat lesser players and cause an upset here and there but it's limited, and net-game and all-court players prey on it.

You need to be strong and sound, not mild and sound. An opposing net-game player usually serves faster and an all-court player volleys better, so take your share of the attack with stronger groundstrokes. Your opponent has to feel they're dangerous to him.

SERVING

Set Yourself Up

Serve calmly. You don't have to coordinate your serve with a continual or spasmodic net approach and there is only a short interval between a first-service fault and your second ball. Serving calmly helps to keep your head up and your right side back until you have hit the ball.

Serve strongly, letting your right leg swing over the baseline for weight and follow-through, and step smoothly into the court. Then press down on the ball of your right foot and return behind your baseline. You'll then be alert and balanced and in your best baseline position before your serve has landed, no matter how hard you hit it. If it's returned it's coming to your strength, your groundstrokes. Feel you've set yourself up.

Power

If you lack power, make sure you're hitting right through the ball with a free wrist. You always do that when practicing, but in a match you can easily half-halt with a stiff wrist at the moment of impact. No amount of trying harder improves things. You have to *know* that even in the tightest match a free wrist and long contact between ball and strings is safer than playing with a tight wrist, which seems to match the occasion. Remember how you throw a ball.

For more power, bend your elbow deeply. For even more, get that *sideways*, not front-on, feeling. Feel that you're serving with a wide arc of your racket head—instead of with a small arc of your wrist for compactness.

Once you have power you can always serve freely past the net (your first priority anyway), so that any adjusting you do is to make the ball land in court.

Adjustments

If your sliced serve won't curve no matter how hard you try, you're hitting the back of the ball. Hit the outside of it.

If your topspin serve won't drop, hit strongly *upwards* at the ball. *You* make it *spin*, and *it* will attend to its own drop.

Although you don't swing at a ball that slips out of your hand and goes wide, you do serve from balls that stray a little from the exact spot of your normal throw. The serve often misses, and it misses in a regular fashion. Know and master your own instant adjustment.

For example, you have a sliced serve and you mean to throw the ball in front of your right shoulder, but this time you throw it in front of your head. Instantly, hit it higher than you were going to—because it won't go as fast and will have more topspin on it and will land in the net. If you have a topspin serve and normally throw the ball over your head, but this time you throw it a little farther to your right, instantly aim lower (less net clearance). You won't get your normal amount of topspin on it and it in turn won't drop as much and will go out.

Bouncing the ball before you serve is not an adjustment, but merely a fad that becomes a habit. It doesn't accustom you to the speed of the ball, and you don't need settling down or whipping up all match long. Similarly, unless you're a two-handed player it's only an inconvenient fad to serve with only one ball. You're not as handless as that.

When you've got the serve, let your opponent feel you want to get at him. If you're always putting it off you give him the initiative and psychologically he's waiting to get at you.

AGAINST A NET-GAME PLAYER

RECEIVING GAMES

A net-game player is most positive when he's serving, playing his serve-and-volley game. Take him on, knowing it's the best he has to offer.

Clear the Decks

Don't stand well behind the baseline and carefully recover his first serves; don't stand so far inside it that your returns are often mis-hit and slow, and don't block the ball in an upward path. All these things give him a comfortable first volley, after which he's in the driver's seat.

If your opponent's a strong player of some repute, don't shut your eyes and slash at the fast first balls of his famous serve or take an out-of-balance swing at his second. That may look like going down fighting, but it's only trying to get everything over and done with in one way or another instead of doing your best. Unforced errors are even better for your opponent than comfortable first volleys.

When playing against any net-game server don't feel down

in a hole, or small, or that you're at the downhill end of a sloping court. Each of these attitudes makes the net seem a long way away and high, and your opponent higher again. Don't stand flat-footed or you'll never get behind a wider ball, and don't teeter about on your toes or you'll get cramps.

Don't bend double, sweeping your racket and your nose widely from side to side. You'll wear yourself out for nothing, because before he serves you've got to stand up in your proper receiving position.

Play Short

Stand on the balls of your feet (which naturally makes you bend your knees a little and lean forward slightly) with the intention that no matter where the serve comes you will get behind it and play *your* shot against it as though your net-game opponent had presented you with your first opportunity to attack. Discount any odd ace and get back on the job.

See the net band as being *low*, and yourself as taking the ball above net height and playing it down and short, whether by topspin drive or chip. Fast or slow, your object is to play down into the dirt. Within volleying reach, a ball needs to be low; crosscourt pass, it needs to be low or it will clear the sideline; down-the-line pass, it lands more safely inside the baseline. Keep shortness in mind and keep confident that you're trying to play the right game.

The only exception to shortness is where you play down the line from a wide serve, because here a long shot allows you to play well beyond the net-man's reach. (See Illus. 32 on next page.)

Vary Your Receiving Position

If, in spite of your efforts, your net-game opponent is getting the better of things and holding his service, vary your receiving position. Stand on the baseline, sometimes inside it and sometimes behind it, but with attack in mind wherever you stand.

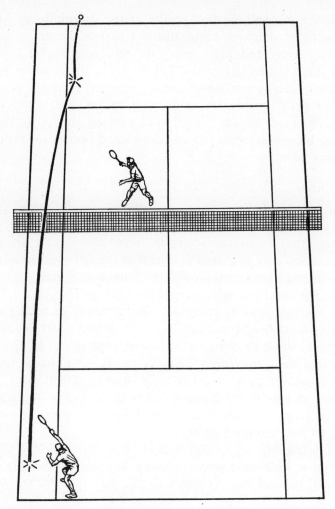

Illus. 32. (see opposite page).

Standing back gives him more time to advance, but on the other hand it allows you more time to get behind the ball for a good solid hit. Don't stand so far back, though, that you have to hit the ball from below net height.

Vary your lateral position too. For example, in the left court sometimes stand farther over to your left, risking the center-line ace (which few players can serve when suddenly called upon) and threatening to attack with your topspin forehand.

Although your backhand may be solid, be prepared to step around it every time you can and hit your forehand. Your forehand may be your less reliable side when rallying against another baseliner, but with nothing to lose against an attacking net-game player it improves vastly. You'll want to play it and you should play it.

Your backhand can't escape though, wherever you stand and however much you're prepared to run around it, when a left-hander is curving his serve away from you in the left court. The same holds true if you're a left-hander and a right-hander is doing the same thing in the right court. Against this type of serving, be prepared to play a backhand. Stand well over near the sideline and hold your racket with your backhand grip. There will be some center-line serves, of course, but you have

Illus. 32. (opposite page) DOWN-THE-LINE PASSING SHOT CURVING INWARDS. Aim over the net *outside* the sideline, beyond the net man's reach. The longer the shot, the farther out of reach it can be—until the ball finally crosses the sideline and lands in court. The ball is farthest out of reach and safest for regaining the court (and you will feel compact in making the stroke) if you turn well sideways and hit outside the ball (with roll or slice) as for a crosscourt shot. This shot is not confined to service returns, but from backhand or forehand is the key to down-the-line passes from wide balls. Without it, your attempts are chopped off by the net player. It turns your opponent's wide approach shots from pressure shots against you into likely disasters for him.

to play the better odds. A curving left-hander won't become bored with serving to your perhaps solid but only half-guarded and half-prepared backhand side in the left court and winning point after point from it. He'll go on doing it till the cows come home.

In Summary

Recognize that your net-game opponent's first serve is your main hurdle and that mere steadiness against it won't do. Allow for plenty of errors, in return for getting a few successes in a row that will lead to a service break—which net-game players with lesser groundstrokes hate.

Get your reward for your attacking tactics when your opponent has to serve his second ball, where you're right in the attacking groove and the serve is slower. Expose your forehand side, sometimes, to a second serve and always be prepared to step around the ball. He can't produce a second-service ace every time he'd like to.

Decide you're doing the right thing and let your strong counterattacking frame of mind take care of your match temperament.

SERVING GAMES

Now that he can't serve-and-volley, your opponent is a reduced figure. Make him join you in a groundstroke game; the whole basis of match tactics is to play your strength against your opponent's weakness as much as possible.

Get as many first serves in as you can; your opponent stands farther back to receive them, and so is physically less ready to attack; mentally, too, he's less prepared to make a moving-in service return against a first ball than against a second. Don't serve your second ball short, allowing him to move into it, run the ball over the net and arrive there himself a second later—in a better position than he had with his serve and first volley. After a service return you want him to stay at the baseline.

Keep him there. You have the stronger groundstrokes to control that, and to win most of the points. Play the ball deep (he can't approach from a long way back, it takes too much time); play the ball with good net clearance (for depth without excessive effort); play it calmly (you're in control); play it wide (so that he can't get behind it and be in balance to approach); play it from corner to corner (a net player runs up to the net all day at his own choosing but dislikes being made to run from side to side). Do whatever you like, but don't lose concentration and play short or mis-hit and play short.

Suspect His Forehand

You're entitled to suspect a net-game player's forehand, no matter what style it is, as possibly being his weakness. Since he bases his game on the volley, he usually makes a sound underspin backhand groundstroke as a somewhat longer version of his backhand volley—but a forehand drive is nothing like a forehand volley and is often the net player's outside chance.

Many a net-game player comes to the net for the dual reason that he volleys well and that he wants to avoid playing his forehand. When your groundstrokes are outgunning his, he resorts to coming in on inadquate shots, and you can take these opportunities to turn his would-be volleying attack into desperate net-covering.

Getting tired, he's likely to play short. Hit deeply and come in for a few winning volleys yourself. That's likely to turn his defeat into a rout.

ALL-COURT OPPONENT

Receiving His Serve

Since an all-court player sometimes follows his serve to the net and sometimes doesn't, you need to play both short and deep returns—but that's not as difficult as it sounds.

After an opponent has served to you several times, following in and remaining back, you can tell by the look of him which

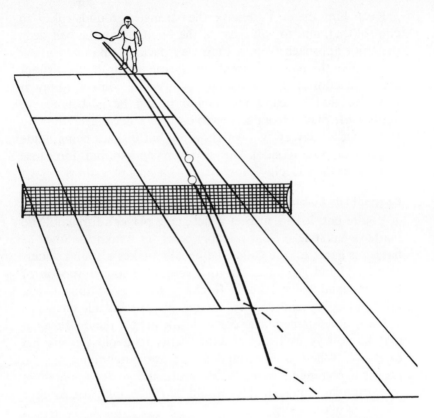

Illus. 33. NET CLEARANCE. When hit from waist high and behind the baseline, a net-skimming shot will land shorter than you wanted it to.

he's going to do. With a first serve to your backhand in the left court expect him to come in. You'll always have time to lengthen your return if he doesn't.

When he follows in, attack. Aim short and low, whether with topspin dip or slow underspin, but with some form of attack in mind. When you miss, don't blame yourself for not having merely kept the ball in play, giving your opponent a chance to miss it. That sounds like percentage tennis, but it's percentage tennis favoring your opponent. Comfortable first volleys are what he comes in for.

When You're Both Rallying

An all-court player is always looking for an approach shot, so keep him back, rallying.

He may not have a weak forehand, but yours is probably better. He usually has a sliced backhand, because most net-seeking players don't have time for rolled shots on both sides. If yours is rolled, baseline to baseline it's stronger than his.

Play strongly and hit deep and stay in control. If you force him well back go for a crosscourt winner or near winner.

Safety Margin

Play with net clearance for safety margin and to avoid playing short. (See Illus. 33.) From a waist- or net-high ball, net clearance should be from two to four feet, depending on speed and roll, but to get it properly in your mind you should stand beside the net post again and watch two hard hitters in action. Probably your own net clearance should be higher than you may have pictured.

For sideline safety-margin allow more than a foot, especially crosscourt, and allow more than a yard for the baseline. When you miss a line by half an inch, see it as having missed by your intended safety margin *plus* that half inch. That way you're less likely to be upset about bad luck. The real error lay in your having missed the right ball-and-strings contact by the merest fraction, so on the next point concentrate on correcting *that*— and play the better for it. An attitude like that stops you from losing more points in sympathy with your "bad luck." With older players it's called experience; no doubt it is, but you don't have to be old to know it.

Flat strokes permit more depth than topspin shots. Although topspin makes a ball drop into court that otherwise would have gone just out, it often leads you to play short unthinkingly.

Decide what the rallying safety-margins for your own strokes should be, and do decide on this or you may rally aimlessly.

But don't be too easy on yourself. Hitting too high over the net all the time allows your opponent to come in and volley. Aiming too far inside the baseline or sideline gives your opponent a short ball or one he can easily get behind, enabling him to play an approach shot from either. Doubling your safety doesn't double your success percentage. It lessens it; too safe becomes too easy.

Play as you'd like to play: strong, hard and deep, keeping most of the groundstroke attack, and putting your opponent on the run when you play for the sidelines with a safety margin in mind. If you don't win with that sort of rallying you have to improve your game, not change to "safety" softness.

WHEN HE'S GOT THE NET

Now it's his turn. From a short ball he's closed in to his best net position—a better one than his halfway service/first-volley position well back—and he's poised to volley.

Whenever this occurs, never play a nothing-shot with the wish that he may somehow miss it. Play a positive shot of one kind or another, as outlined below.

Outright Winner

If he hurried his approach shot and hit it shorter than he meant to, go for a winner. You won't get as good a chance again during that point.

Lob

If he's not making the mistake of sitting right on top of the net, but is still aggressively close, you've a better chance of making him play a defensive overhead than of passing him, especially if you're playing against the breeze. If possible, make him play a backhand overhead—and anticipate that he will almost certainly play this crosscourt to your backhand

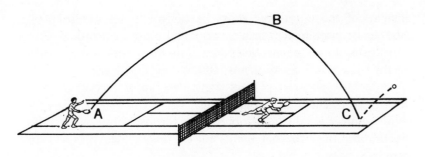

Illus. 34. DIRECT LOB CLEARANCE. Aim at B, somewhere beyond the net man's reach, instead of trying to land the ball at C. Supporters of this method say that B is nearer than C and more in line with the upward direction of their stroke. Non-supporters say that it only makes them hit the ball out; they'd rather aim for the end of their lob, at C. Try anything rather than lob short, the game's horror shot.

side. If he's left-handed his shot is again likely to come to your backhand side—because it's your weaker side which most left-handers have accustomed themselves to attack with their backhand overheads.

If he covers your lob with his forehand overhead, again expect the ball to be played to your backhand. If he's left-handed, the flat racket face used for a fading-back smash will probably make him smash towards your forehand side. See Illus. 21 again. In any case, all left-handers, other than those who specialize in a sliced service, have a strong preference for smashing to their off side, your forehand.

You can see at once if your opponent, right-handed or left, is unsound overhead. He covers your lob awkwardly and winds up with his full service action; he hits at great speed and (if right-handed) aims for your forehand sideline with an angled racket face, etc. He will probably miss, but even if he manages to smash a winner, you know a lucky shot when you see one. In similar circumstances, lob again. He will then keep farther back from the net and will have to make defensive volleys instead of the aggressive shots he originally set out to play. Sooner or later he'll return to his usual close-in position. You lob again. Anyone who gives you a lobbing opportunity early in the match will do so again later.

Unsound overhead players don't deserve to receive a short lob. If you believe in net clearance, believe in lob clearance—either indirectly, through lobbing for the backline, or directly, by lobbing over the net man's racket-reach. (See Illus. 34 on previous page.)

Keep lobs well in mind in every game played against the wind. The wind cushion allows you to hit them strongly—whereas it reduces the speed of your passing shots.

Many tall players have a wide reach for volleys and a short one for smashes. The explanation is that they base their net game on chopping off passing shots, and they squeeze in too close to the net.

Backhand over the Center Strap

An all-court opponent's most usual form of pouncing on a short service return from the right court is to play it fairly deep to your backhand corner, safely within the sideline, and come to the net. From there he cuts off your down-the-line backhand with a forehand crosscourt volley as a winner-in-one, or else he punches it straight down the line behind your backhand. Next time, you try to keep your shot lower, only to hit the tape. The net's high at the sides, 3' 6". All-court players win countless points from that type of attack.

It's natural for you to choose to play down the line. It's the open side, where you can see space, and you can't see it crosscourt through the net man's body. You can't hit crosscourt across his body and out of his reach without going over the far sideline, and you can't lob because he can cover it with a forehand smash. So you hit a down-the-line backhand—and he cuts it off.

His position seems impregnable, but it's not. Hit hard and

as low as you can straight over the center band. That gives him a fast ball to low volley or half volley, and nearly always you'll still be in the game.

After a couple of these experiences he will move in closer to avoid low volleying. Don't change to down the line. Lob.

Wide Passing Shot

If you can get your racket and your weight *behind* the ball (not inside it), the wider your opponent's approach shot is, the more open the court is to your passing shot. See Illus. 32 again, where a wide ball allowed you to use an area not even within your opponent's court.

So, when your opponent has the net after making a wide approach shot do not see him as a dominating figure who has you on the run, but see yourself as only having to get there to have a passing shot set up.

Mark-Time Shots

Your opponent has played the Center Theory and taken the net. You can't pass him in one shot, so you play a mark-time shot first. Roll the ball (low and dipping) to either side of him or even in front of him, making him low volley or half volley, and you will stay in the game. You can slice the ball low to any of these positions, but that calls for light touch. Probably, the stronger hit roll feels safer.

A second mark-time shot is a very high lob—a vertical type that will make the net man let it bounce, thus taking him away from the net. He may dispatch it, but may play another approach shot from it that isn't as good as the first. You can't expect him to miss it.

Half Drive

His Center-Theory shot lands the ball straight at your feet. Throw your weight forward in a strong half volley with topspin over and outside the ball. Compared to Illus. 17, your weight is much more forward and the shot is hard-working, not effortless.

Although the outside spin always sends your shot crosscourt, it allows extra control—and without a crosscourt arm action your forward-only arm action may not be strong enough to hit in any other direction. Unless your opponent is used to playing this shot himself he may not anticipate that its direction will be crosscourt, and with a strong shot you have a chance of staying in the game.

Hitting Yourself out of Trouble

His Center-Theory shot is even more awkward, landing short of your feet and a little towards your forehand side—while you're leaning back with no hope of getting forward to play a half volley close to the ground. You'll have to play a shot that's somewhere between a half volley and a rising ball. If you try to lob, a mis-hit will be fatal.

Hit yourself out of trouble. Get all the backswing you can —you're leaning back so can't get any body weight into your shot—and hit as hard as you can. From your leaning back and hitting your hardest the ball wants to fly high and all the way to the back fence, so as you hit you have to drag it down. Hit over and around the ball with strong covering topspin and pull it crosscourt with long contact between ball and strings. Make it a fine piece of racket work while you're at it, by deliberately hitting above center on your strings (see Illus. 2 again); this adds to your control of an awkward and hard-hit shot.

So, even against your opponent's most effectively placed Center Theory you can play two mark-time shots, a "half drive" and a fast drag-control shot. That's counterattack.

Center-Band Recovery

This is a last-chance shot.

Your opponent's approach shot or one of his volleys is so short and wide that you have to scramble to get your racket under the ball before it bounces twice. He's ready to stand over any down-the-line shot, a crosscourt is an impossible angle and you're too close to him to get a lob over his head.

With your momentum, run the ball (you can hardly hit it) as hard as you can, straight at the intersection of tape and net band. Don't aim above it, since only a few inches of net clearance are enough to give him the easy volley he's expecting. Aim at the tape, relying on a combination of the rising flight of the ball and your own force to escape it by a whisker.

A volleyer sometimes misses these unexpectedly low recoveries, perhaps because the tape covers his view of the ball for a fraction of a second and he thinks it's in the net. Perhaps you may tip the tape and whip the ball over his racket.

It could be called luck, but luck sticks to a player who's hard to beat.

Backhand with Eastern Forehand Grip

This is another last-ditch shot, made against a volley he has punched so far behind your backhand that normally you could only hit the ball towards the near side fence.

Swing your right foot right around towards your baseline and take a long step after the ball, completely turning your back to the net. With an Eastern forehand grip, keep your wrist low as a pivot point and flick your racket head around the ball. Hit hard from a strong and flexible wrist, because you haven't any power from weight or swing. If your shot is to go in at all it can only be down-the-line, low or lobbed— because if you can hit it crosscourt the ball couldn't have been so *completely* behind you after all.

AGAINST OTHER BASELINERS

CUT PLAYERS

A cut player often merely looks self-taught, but he is likely to beat an unwary driver. He is usually supremely steady. Having only a small stroke to play on either forehand or backhand, his timing is easy and there is little to go wrong. The height of the ball's bounce does not matter to him, since he can cut under low ones and into medium ones, and down and round high ones to some extent. Cutting the ball gives a degree of long contact between ball and strings, so he has good control.

However, little attempted, little gained, and the cut player lacks power. He also often mis-hits against fast balls, because he hits at the ball with an angled racket face and never a full one.

He can break up your game in two ways, first through your unaware stroking, and later, if need be, by breaking up your pattern of play.

He begins by merely getting the ball into play and letting you make mistakes.

● LOW BOUNCE—The cut he puts on the ball makes it bounce lower than usual. In the early stages you may hit a number of shots in the net.

● SLOW BOUNCE—His underspin makes the ball bounce slower than usual. You may hit too early, contacting the ball in the upward part of your swing and hitting it out.

● BACKSPIN ON THE BALL—Your topspin does not bite into backspin (as it does into opposing topspin) and so it does not spin the ball as much and your shot may go out. Against backspin you can lose your "solid" feel.

However, if you understand spin a cut holds no terrors for you and mainly gives you a slow bounce that is easy to time and to hit if you take care. On a fast surface it may skid more quickly, but even then the total stroke (flight plus bounce) is considerably slower from a cut than from a drive.

In rallying against cut strokes do *not* follow a possibly half-understood maxim, "Reply to a cut with a cut." That gives the best controlling spin, but you would be playing your opponent's game and inviting defeat at it. Use a cut whenever you want to, and that's all.

Breaking Up Your Pattern

When you're hitting the ball into play your weight of stroke is too much for the cut player, and to survive he must break up the pattern of your driving rallies.

He refuses to rally with you, beyond a shot or two, in the normal way of exchanging evenly paced well-placed shots. Instead, he continually changes his pace, sometimes introducing shots that are almost lobs. He follows a high-bouncing shot by one carrying all the spin he can muster and clinging low to the court's surface. He plays drop-shots.

He plays long and short, first using a long dropped-head inside-underspin drive to your backhand corner and following it with a short crosscourt cut. He comes to the net now and then, as a surprise move to catch an easy ball.

Playing like that and winning, he's being a match-player to his fingertips—but only within his stroke limitations.

Cutting Is Not Strong Enough

You must not feel that you are in the hands of a master player and tactician who puts the ball wherever he wants to at whatever speed and spin he chooses and who seldom makes a mistake. You must not feel that you are all style and he is all effectiveness, when in truth his stroke limitation makes him more like a hooked fish who's making a fight of it, but will be reeled in in the end.

His change of pace is only downwards, towards playing yet more slowly, because he hasn't got the power to go up the scale and increase it. When he lobs the ball over the net don't lose your head and try to drive a winner from it. That's not easy to do, because you have to change from steadily driving a ball that's coming directly towards your racket face to driving hard at one dropping down from a high bounce, at an angle to your racket's path. (Reduce this angle as much as possible by always taking your racket back high against a high bounce.)

No one can count on winning with a succession of drop-shots. When not almost perfect they either land in the net or else go too far and merely become short balls. The drop-shot is a spectacular winner every now and again, but once your opponent has alerted you to his likely use of drop-shots he needs to make them with finer and finer touch—and he ends as the loser. Drop-shot users are well advised to quit while they're ahead.

An underspin-drive can only be penetrating when played "going-away" to your backhand side, and it is always telegraphed. The following crosscourt cut can only be slow, because it has no topspin dip to allow it to be fast. It may be fast enough, though, if you return the ball too high and allow your opponent to make his forehand cut as a downward stroke with curving outside-sidespin.

Expect him to come to the net sometimes. Then play as you do against all-court players, who confront you with more difficult shots because they're not counting on any surprise. And they're better volleyers, as well.

Don't be impatient. Use your superior weight of stroke. Though you may be a baseliner, come to the net and volley.

Cut Player Yourself

A down wind helps your shots gain the speed they lack, and you have the necessary steadiness and accuracy. Try to hold every down-wind game you play, as though it were a service game, and try to break one from the other end.

You're a reliable player who seldom plays badly, but probably you realize that your strokes prevent you from improving further. If you want to cross your present barrier you'll have to give up some of your steadiness for more weight. Change your small cuts to longer slices, or take the ball earlier and approach and become an all-court player, or develop a rolled forehand.

You may not have any barrier. You may be champion of your district or your age group or of anything else and enjoy playing your game as it is. You may have a lot more tricks up your sleeve, too, than have been mentioned here. If that's true and I have been unfair to your cut-stroke game or given you unwanted advice—your pardon, please.

TWO-HANDERS

When playing an opponent whose two-handed backhand is a short solid block, don't hit your first serve into this rock-like stroke. Don't waste your energy like that. As you are not a following-in net man, he can play it steadily back without error.

When the two-hander is the player's outstanding strength and the best shot on the court, rally to the other side with the feeling that you're overcoming a weaker player's forehand rather than that you're fearfully avoiding your opponent's demolishing two-hander. He would like to run round the ball, but since double-handedness impedes this his weaker side is not difficult to find. When the time comes, play wide of his two-hander—which you may have almost shut out of his game, but now bring in at a disadvantage.

Know Each Type

Your opponent serves with his right hand, plays two-handed on his right side and has a single-handed left-handed forehand —so you type him as a right-hander with all his eggs in one basket in that two-handed right-handed forehand of his. You plan to concentrate your attack on that defenseless left-side forehand—only you find it powerful, better than his two-hander. For a moment you feel disorientated.

Recover your balance quickly. Look at his serve again, and see that it's awkwardly made. He's a left-hander serving with his right (wrong) hand, for some reason best known to himself. At once you're re-orientated. Don't be annoyed with him, because he'd serve much better against you now if he'd begun left-handed.

AMBIDEXTROUS OPPONENT

This player has two single-handed forehands, the stronger one normally being on his serving side.

His reach against wide balls is better than that of any other player, but he's weak against balls played fast and straight at him, particularly when anywhere near the net. However, with the increase in double-handers some ambidextrous players now use two-handed strokes for shots close to the body. Since shots close to the body are a two-hander's strength this type of player may seem to have a strength for everything.

It certainly seems so when he beats you. But with right hand, left hand, double-handed backhand, cross-handed forehand and perhaps even wrong-handed serve, surely he's got too many hands all over the place to have any strength anywhere.

It certainly seems so when you beat him.

FOREHAND-STRENGTH LEFT-HANDERS

To find this type of left-hander's protected backhand, first play to his forehand side. (See Illus. 35.)

If you are the left-hander you need to recognize your opponent's first shot as being preparatory, and then play strongly against it to prevent the second (to your backhand) from being damaging. Try to take charge of the rally at this point if you can. You have two good shots to do it with. (See Illus. 36.)

Right-hander, never play down-the-line from your forehand corner to a left-hander's forehand, exposing your backhand to those attacking crosscourt forehands of his which he can hit with such certainty. That's as ill-advised as an all-court player coming in on a short nothing-ball. Your preparatory shot is better made as a crosscourt backhand, deep or wide, or a forehand from nearer the center of your baseline. You can hit any of these three shots strongly, since you're using the strokes you've used for most of your tennis life to attack right-handers' backhands.

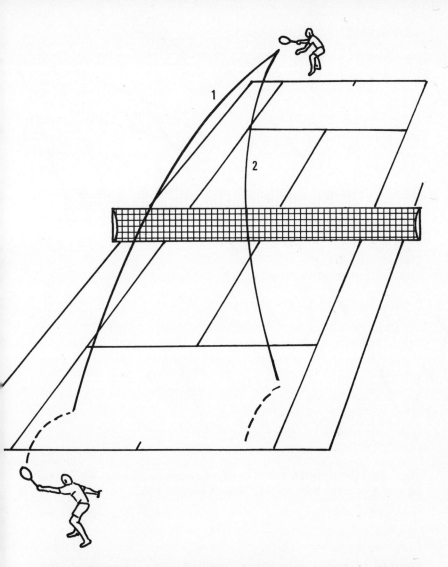

Illus. 35. FINDING A LEFT-HANDER'S BACKHAND. Obvious in diagram, but not necessarily so on court. You can lose a match before thinking of these tactics.

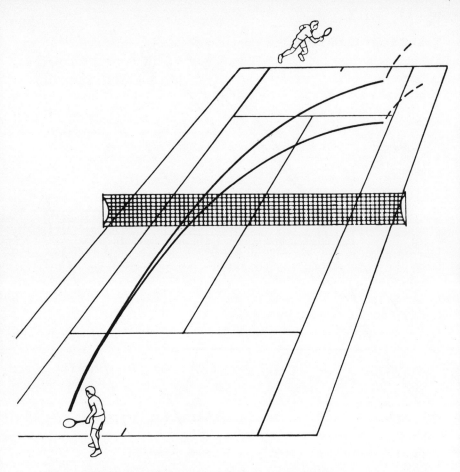

Illus. 36. LEFT-HANDER TAKES OVER. As a left-hander, you have either of your two stock balls to play, almost without risk.

EXTREME EASTERN (See Appendix 1)

Be prepared for an EE opponent to be the right-handed equivalent of a typical left-hander, and one who will demolish your preparatory shot to his forehand if it is high-bouncing.

However, in comparison with the left-hander a right-handed EE player's backhand is easier to find, since you play your straight forehand and crosscourt backhand into it. Don't make the mistake, though, of thinking these two shots are all you need. They may work well at the start of the match and give you a good lead, but by constantly playing them you play your opponent's backhand into form, while at the same time he hardly needs to move.

EE players don't like your having a strong crosscourt forehand up your sleeve, as a preparatory shot or as a winner whenever he leaves his forehand side too open.

CONTINENTAL AND WESTERN

Continental players and Western players with Western backhands have only one thing in common: good balance between forehand and backhand strengths. From there they are extreme opposites, the Continental players liking the ball low and wide and the Western high and close.

Against a Westerner your tactics are to play the ball behind him. A copy-book example is to play your backhand (crosscourt, low, short and wide) away from his backhand; then, when he returns your shot, you play deep behind his forehand.

Continental players often look classy, an older one looking like an ex-champion and a younger one a coming star. They look good because they play balls that are low and away from the body so freely, and that's where tennis looks its smoothest. In rallying, many prefer to hit their forehand drives at knee height rather than waist height. That's below net height, but they feel they get more power from a somewhat *downward* forward swing at this lower ball.

Downwards is associated with the Continental grip. It is the strongest grip for hitting downwards, whether you're hammering a nail, chopping wood with a tomahawk, or serving or slicing a ball with a racket. For hitting a plain forehand forwards, it's the weakest grip.

Therefore, it's no test of a Continental player's forehand to see him hitting low balls well. In the warm-up play some high ones. If his forehand is weak against them your most effective means of rallying when the match starts is to roll your drives high over the net with topspin, giving the ball a high topspin bounce.

You're Continental . . .

Avoid being forced into playing this shoulder-height game, where you're over-concerned with controlling the ball and unable to do much else. In your earlier days you could let the ball drop to your favored height, but better-class opponents now hit the ball too deep for you to do that without going too far back altogether.

Develop rising-ball play. At first do this for your own protection, but when you're good at it it becomes the most penetrating baseline rallying there is, without even looking aggressive.

. . . and Better on the Backhand

While you're building up your forehand your backhand is your stronger side, and you must try not to reveal this early in a match. Conceal it, by winning points with your backhand as unobtrusively as possible. For example, after a rally of a few shots your opponent's court may become wide open for a backhand crosscourt winner from you; make your winner by merely putting the ball there, instead of revealing a strong and polished shot that your forehand could never equal.

Let your opponent believe your backhand is no more than solid and let him lose against it.

In rallying, whenever the ball lands in front of you step to your left and play a forehand. People run miles round their backhands and that's commonplace, but if you show the slightest tendency to step round your forehand it's a dead giveaway. Near the end of a match you have to play the best shot you can, but that's different from showing your hand before you have to.

Many opponents with strong forehands themselves just can't believe that anyone else's forehand is not better than their (unobtrusive) backhand.

ROBUST BASELINE TACTICS

The basis of tactics is to use your strength as much as possible and attack your opponent's weaknesses all the time—but good Continental, Australian and Eastern-style opponents often don't offer you a worthwhile stroke weakness to attack.

You're supposed to unsettle your opponent and break up his game by mixing up your shots—but that only applies if you can play that sort of controlled game. If, like many another baseliner, your game is heavily based on robust driving, you well know that you're more effective keeping to that rather than trying to vary your play with shots that aren't as good. In the latter case, all you do is to let your *opponent's* robust driving take over.

"Vary your length. Bring him in with a short one, then toss over his head." Like most hard drivers you find this advice difficult to carry out, and on a hard surface, useless anyway. All you serve up is a short ball.

All this doesn't mean that there's no place for tactics in your game. Even when you are opposed to a baseliner similar to yourself—having a solid forehand and backhand and a game based on hitting the ball hard and often—there's most certainly a place for tactics. To begin with, see Illus. 36 again, for a clear example of diagonals defeating down-the-line play.

Diagonals

You have the better position if you play deep crosscourt shots and your opponent prefers playing his shots deep down the

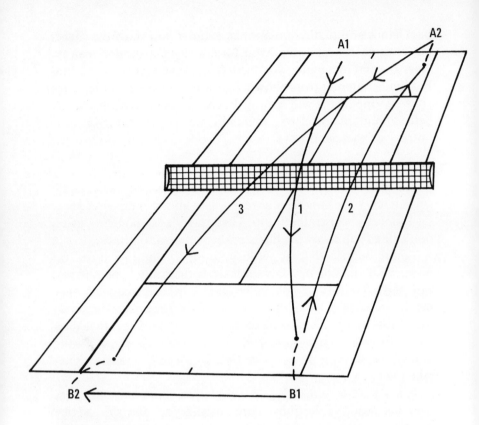

Illus. 37. DIAGONALS. You (A) begin your combination with an attacking crosscourt forehand drive (1) to your opponent's forehand corner. From B1 he should not return down the line, but almost invariably does (2). You play (3) and he begins his chase. If he then plays his backhand down the line from B2, you play another long diagonal forehand to his forehand corner. Although his strokes may be as good as yours, you've got him in perpetual motion.

line. The bounces of your shots carry towards his sidelines, and often beyond them when you hit with outside-topspin, and his stay within yours. He has more distance to cover before getting the ball and balancing himself for his shot, all the time. He's chasing the ball, while you're only taking a few steps to play it. (See Illus. 37.)

Your opponent is not forced to use his shot no. 2 down the line but it is entirely natural for him to do so: it takes less effort than getting farther behind the ball to hit it crosscourt; a straight forehand is his better shot; he's playing the ball to your backhand; he knows he must not play a short crosscourt and leave himself stranded in the corner, so he does the opposite and plays deep down the line. Watch a match for yourself and see how often shot no. 2 is played in reply to shot no. 1.

Your opponent is not necessarily aware of your deadly-diagonal tactics. When you play shot no. 3, he may think you've got a good backhand and so next time he'll hit harder and deeper and try to make you miss it. If that's his thinking, his next-time will be down the line again.

NOTE: When an opponent plays shot no. 1 to you, make the effort to get as far as you can behind the ball and play it back in a crosscourt direction to land about a yard or so on the forehand side of his center mark. Hit it fairly high and fairly slowly, for depth and for time to let you get back to the center of your baseline before he hits the ball again. Few baseliners follow in a shot they've played to your forehand.

Referring to Illus. 37 again, your opponent's backhand from position B2 is not shown, but he may be forced to play it down the line to your forehand by the speed and depth of shot no. 3 and by his long chase for it from B1 to B2, corner to corner. However, when a penetrating shot like no. 3 is not available to you, you can induce your opponent to play his backhand down the line, your intention being to set up a forehand diagonal. (See Illus. 38 on next page.)

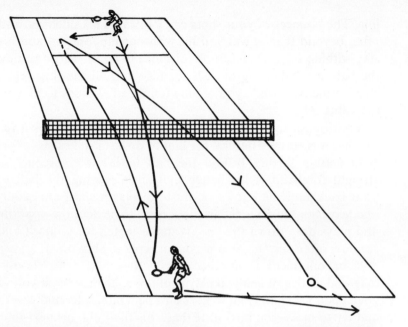

Illus. 38. SETTING UP A DIAGONAL. Step around your backhand and play a forehand to your opponent's backhand corner, inducing him to hit down the line to your somewhat open forehand side. Then play a long diagonal forehand to his forehand corner, which has opened more widely.

Play this move again and again.

Your forehand and backhand driving is often about equal to your opponent's. These robust tactics (not calling for touch or change of pace or different spin—none of which may suit your game) can enable you to play all over him.

6. WHAT TO EXPECT IN THE MATCH

THE WARM-UP

It's the night before. When you toss on a sleepless bed, you think about starting the match with your serve and having to land the ball in a tiny service box, or else you're playing a match point. You worry about how you'll *play*, how you'll hit the ball.

Well, think about how you'll hit the ball in the warm-up. That's the next time you'll *play*, and no one minds facing a warm-up.

It's your last meal. It's here that you wonder if your nerves will let you play your *real* game. Well, think about the tactics you'll probably use, and what type or style your opponent may be. Interest lessens nervousness about abstractions.

It's time to go on the court. Don't drift onto it—realizing much later that your footwork is sluggish. Press your toes strongly against the surface. Walk a little pigeon-toed for strength if you want to, not enough for anyone to notice. Press your thumb into the balls you'll use. New, they always feel about the same, but do it anyway. If they are once-used, you'll know the pressure and the look of their cloth. Ping your racket and strings hard on the butt of your hand and listen to the note, and if it's a cold day blow warmly into your palm. You'll have the feel of your racket handle and almost the feel of ball on strings before you've even hit a shot. Determine which way the wind is blowing, however lightly.

It's time to hit the first couple of balls. If your opponent is known as a great player or hard hitter or whatever, take up a net position first. From here you can easily match him whoever he is, and that settles you down and smartens you up right from the start. To others, you're practicing your volleys first, that's all. Ask for a few lobs. Time them, and stretch yourself out.

Groundstroke time. Consciously watch the ball and get hold of it by hitting slightly outside it on forehand and backhand so that there's no off-side spraying to lower your confidence. Hit every ball *over* the net as the quickest way to find your feel and range. If the first few go out, hit the next ones with strong long-contact and *make* them land in. Work reasonably hard, trying to get every ball on the first bounce and get warm. Whenever you pick a ball up to put it into play once more, hit it with the short-shoulder serve action you use for smashing and make the contact a solid smack.

At the same time get to know your opponent. Renew your interest in him now that he's performing for you, which again lessens your nervousness as the start of the match nears. You're going to beat *him*, not play strokes for onlookers' applause. (There goes a great load off your mind: self-consciousness.)

Serving time now. Practice your serve with at least two balls in your hand, serving firsts and seconds. Serve from both sides and finish with the right, where you'll begin. Serving time over, the last thing you say to yourself—whether your opponent is unknown or famous or you're supposed to win—is that you're going to be hard to beat. Unless outclassed, you will be, nervous or not.

Starting. It's your serve. Don't jerk your throwing arm outwards, throwing the ball too far forward and beginning everything with a right-side collapse. Bring your arm up comfortably closer to your body, bend your elbow and hit with a free wrist and long contact and send the ball over the net. It goes out. Hit the second with more spin; it curves or drops into court. You're on your way.

Receiving. Be alert to get behind the ball and then hit it with long contact over the net, starting with a good solid feel. You're on your way.

Match point. When it comes it's nothing like last night's dream. Never bears the remotest resemblance.

Win or lose. Win, you may not be satisfied with your strokes, but the win comforts you. Lose, it was nowhere nearly as bad or disappointing as you'd feared. "Nearly had my game right. Next time . . ."

Remember that the warm-up always comes first. It's much better then.

SPINNING FOR — WHAT?

It's called spinning for serve or tossing for serve, but match players like to have a wider choice than that.

Serve

In normal circumstances, choose to serve. Throughout a set it's better to be a game ahead and your opponent's serve to break, than a game down and your own serve to hold. If you win your opponent's first service-game you'll probably lead 3–0 before he serves again. He's only one service-break down but if he doesn't get it quickly his score goes along from 0–3 to 1–4 to 2–5.

Defensively, if you lose your opening service-game and he wins his to make you 0–2 down, at least it's your serve again.

Receive

Choose to receive if you're so confident of winning all your service-games that you only need to break one of his to give you the set—and you reason that that one is most likely to be his first service-game, the opening game of the match, while he's cold (meaning careless, or shaky, or less on the job).

Or, receive if you feel it means you've nothing to lose and everything to gain, because it's his serve and the opening pressure is on him and not you.

Or, receive if you feel under-confident about winning the opening game of the match with your serve and would rather settle down first.

The danger in choosing to receive is that if you lose your own serve in the second game you will probably be down 0–3 before you serve again. It's only one service-break, but you wouldn't have chosen to be there.

End of the Court

If you choose an end your opponent will probably serve, but you can't count on it. He can receive if he wants to. You haven't given him the serve—you have chosen an end, and the next choice (between serving and receiving) is *his*, *not yours*.

Mainly, you take an end in preference to serving or receiving because of sun and wind. Take the bad end and get used to it all through the warm-up and during the first game as well. Then you have two games at the better end, and return to the bad end you're already used to.

Or, take an end if you're in great need of some hard-hitting practice during the warm-up to raise your confidence. Take the end against the breeze.

Giving Your Opponent First Choice

Because this has the same effect as losing the spin, few players realize that it can be of positive benefit to them.

If the most important thing to you is to serve your first service-game from a certain end (say, into a steady cushioning breeze), give your opponent the first choice. He can't refuse to make it. The rules say that you may serve or receive, or take an end, or require your opponent to make the first choice.

The clearest example of getting what you want by giving your opponent the choice occurs at the start of a mixed doubles match with a fairly strong wind blowing. If it is important that the man serves first for his side and that the woman doesn't serve against the wind, the only way you can ensure this happening is to let your opponents choose something first.

Returning to singles, you may have a fast serve that is erratic at first, and have always been secretly glad whenever your opponent won the toss and you could then arrange for your first service-game to be into the breeze. It always can be.

Lost Spin

When your opponent wins the spin and says he'll serve, you can take what you think is the worse end, and have nothing to lose because he's serving, and then have the next two games from the better end.

Or, you can give him the worse end and try to catch his first service-game cold.

When he says he'll receive, you have your serve from whichever end you choose and should feel well treated.

When he chooses an end—almost certainly the bad one—you can serve from the better end and probably lead one-love. It's never too early to start winning.

He is expecting you to serve but you can receive, to catch his service cold at the bad end. That can backfire. If he holds it you've then got two games at the bad end and he could lead 3–0 with his serve to follow.

All Ends Happily

You need to know the fundamentals, but you can see that after that the whole business is shot with if's and but's. The calming aspect is that the winner's choice is not overwhelming and the loser gets a choice also. The important thing is to feel that your choice has set you up with a potential advantage to play towards. Getting an early picture does not interfere with any match-temperament system you may have developed of avoiding crisis points by simply playing for each point, one at a time, without thinking of any game score.

SUN AND WIND SERVING

Sometimes the sun is *directly* in line with the ball when you throw it up for your normal serve. Do *not* serve that way; it blinds you for the service return. Instead, make your throw as close as possible to normal, throwing the ball just beyond the sun's glare.

When you adjust your throw, to right or left of normal, it

will alter your normal serve to some extent. Be content with that, or else use another type of serve that suits the enforced position of your throw. If your normal serve is sliced, you can throw the ball a little to right or left of the sun's direct line and serve more roundhouse or more upright and still feel you're serving a sliced serve—or, you can regard the throw to the left as being your *chosen* position for a topspin-sliced or topspin serve, and serve either of those. See Illus. 13 again, for diagrammatic ball positions.

Practice it. You'll probably find that turning your normal stance either more sideways or more front-on has more effect than taking different positions between sideline and centermark—but you can try combining them. Get yourself settled with a sun-serve so that you use it at once in a match, even if your warm-up is at the other end—instead of marching back and forth along the baselines trying throws from here, there and everywhere. An experienced opponent, seeing these antics, will know that the sun bothers you and will put every service return into play without risk. Learn to cope with the sun.

Don't Bend the Rules

Do not agree if your opponent or an inexperienced umpire or anyone else suggests serving from one end only, until the sun moves out of the way. Bending the rules can bring unthought-of consequences in its wake and ruin a match. For example, if you agree to serving from only the non-sunny end because your opponent wears glasses, he may like serving from wide out (which you never do) and the background from there may be very bad. Or, instead of glasses he may have a fast but erratic serve (while yours is steady), but now he may be serving every game into a cushioning breeze and getting more first balls in than he otherwise would have. Serving from one end also means you'll be *receiving* into the sun all the time—and he may have a high-bouncing American Twist serve and you a low-bouncing sliced one. And so on.

Agree to bending a rule and you'll never be happy if you lose because of it.

Wind

If you've already experienced trouble when serving on windy days you know how nerve-wracking it can be—leaving your match temperament in tatters.

Never regard serving into the wind as a difficulty. The wind is a safety cushion. You can hit harder than normally to increase your confidence, or you can serve with your accustomed rhythm and get about the same speed for your effort by using less controlling spin for curve or dip. Against a strong wind, throw the ball a little more forward, so that it eases back and you can hit it soundly from your usual place. In any case it makes you feel you're leaning well into the ball.

Downwind

When serving downwind (wind blowing behind you), that dreadful feeling of insecurity and panic that attacks so many players is mainly caused by chasing after the ball. Hold your hand a shade closer to your body and throw the ball a shade farther back. Some players say that when serving downwind they concentrate on control and let the speed take care of itself; others that they serve their second ball as their first.

A few say that they aim lower over the net. Though you should use whatever method gives you confidence, you should not take this concept to mean exchanging a safe net clearance for net skimming.

If you can master downwind serving it is a tremendous advance in your game. Your horror end becomes your dominating end. You can also use the speed and going-away direction of a crosswind to serve aces, instead of having to hit into its direction for safety.

Strong Gusts

The most unsafe wind condition is a downwind that is blowing in strong gusts. A short throw is essential. Again, as with sun, you can modify your normal serve to suit this short throw or else you can develop a special stand-by. A suggestion is a topspin serve with its backswing action reduced to a minimum, in which you hit the ball at the top of your throw. Feel you're hitting the ball on the rise if you like, the point being that you're not hitting at it in its wobbling gust-affected descent. It's a compact serve with good net clearance and topspin-arc control. The only thing to go wrong is the normal topspin hazard of mishitting, and the short throw lessens that chance as much as possible.

Free Wrist

In all windy conditions you must continue to serve with a free wrist, long contact and follow through. With a downwind you're inclined to hit with a stiff wrist at contact, for fear of over-hitting the service line, but that's no way to serve with conviction.

All Part of the Party

Tennis isn't usually played in blinding sun and howling gale, but it's usually played outdoors where sun and wind or breeze and irregular bounces now and then are all part of the party. Your opponent is affected as much as you are. To complain instead of *playing* means you're only a fair-weather player.

Think of the rewards. Downwind, aces; upwind, an "automatic serve"; gusts, solidity.

PLAYING THE POINTS

If you don't know how to play the points within a game you're easy to beat. If you do know how to play the points you won't let your opponent off the hook when you're ahead and you won't surrender too easily when you're behind.

The Later Points

Naturally, all game points (even 40–love) occur late in the game, but the term "Later Points" particularly applies to:

• Game points with a one point difference in the score (40–30, 30–40, ad. in, ad. out).

• Points one away from game point with level score or one point difference (deuce, 30–all, 30–15, 15–30).

On these points, play the soundest tactical shot, if possible giving your opponent no chance to make a winner from it. Close the game up.

Leave it to your opponent to risk a loser-in-one with, say, a drop-shot from the back of the court, because he's tired of rallying; or a rather dangerous try for a second-service ace, because he wants the point settled quickly; or a fast crosscourt only inches inside the line attempted as a winner, when safely inside would still have left him in charge of the rally.

Play strongly in closing the game up. If you play tentatively you'll give your opponent a short ball instead of the soundest tactical shot, and he'll take charge from there.

Easier Said Than Done

It's obvious, but even though you know your course you can be distracted from it. For example, you're serving and you win the first point after a long exchange and feel you're getting on top. You want to make it 30–love, and you almost have when he plays a weak shot against your serve—but the ball drops over as a dead net-cord and saves him. In the next point you're in charge of the rally—until he suddenly makes an outrageous fluke. He's robbed you twice of 40–love. Annoyed, you serve a very fast, "He-won't-*touch-this*" first serve (it misses) and then, worse, a "My-turn-for-*some*-of-the-luck" attempted second service ace (it's a double fault).

If you play like that a mistake costs you dearly. The score at 15–30 was your warning point. Ignoring it and sliding all the way to double game point down for a service break is a harsh penalty for one little flutter.

You may look like a strong player and perhaps a hard man, but if you don't play the points in a close match, you're soft to beat.

Too bad if playing the points quenches some of your fieriness. If you play the points *as they stand* it helps you to forget a past mistake or bad luck or other distraction—and that's more than a fair exchange.

Early Stage

It's here that you can afford to vary your game. Varying your game (so that your opponent isn't certain of your shots in the later stage) is not the same thing as being unsound, let alone reckless. You have all sorts of maxims to prevent you from squandering an early point: win the first point and it takes two to pass you; win the second for 30–love, or save it for 15–all; win the third . . .

Thirty-Love

Tennis isn't all doggedness, not all fighting back, not always coming from behind and battling uphill.

Start each new game with the intention of getting to a 30–love and then looking down on the game from there. That's more refreshing than a cool drink, as you change ends in a long and even match.

THE VITAL SEVENTH

The last game is the winning-post, but the most important game on the way to it is the seventh. The winner is usually the set winner. There's nothing magical about any one game, but the seventh is the pivot point. Always be aware of it.

Three-All. Non-awareness by either player is dangerous, because the other one is not likely to be so lax. A careless loser suddenly realizes he is likely to face a 3–5 deficit.

Four-Two Lead. Many a set is lost from here, the leader becoming nervous about leading or vaguely thinking that although he has only two more games to win, the end looks a long way off.

All he should do is bear down on the seventh. Often a match is lost from a 4–2 lead in the third set, the leader not being sure afterwards of exactly how he lost. He could not have been aware of the vital seventh or he would have remembered every point of it. It just passed him by.

Five-One and Your Serve. You relax, and the score goes to 30–40. Then you decide you'd just as soon finish the set on his serve and start the next with your own again. But when he wins and holds his serve and you serve again at 5–3, you're suddenly aware that this is your last chance to win without breaking his serve. You can easily become tentative and hope he'll lose the game for you. He doesn't, though, and you finally get to a tie-breaker. With nothing to lose, because he should have lost long ago, your opponent wins. There were other games you could have won, but you had by far your best chance in the seventh.

You may say that all this makes the seventh a crisis game for you, one you're likely to lose by self-inflicted tension and nervousness while your opponent plays blissfully on. Outbalancing that, you *must* know your position. In playing the points, needless mistakes in the Later Points cost you dearly, and similarly you pay heavily for any lapse of concentration in the vital seventh.

Small Brother

That's the fourth game, in lesser fashion.

Leading 2–1 and opponent serving, don't feel satisfied just to be ahead. You can't lose if you stay ahead, but you've found your form by now and it's time to break through. Three-one is likely to give you four-two, where you'll get your teeth into that seventh.

Logical support for the seventh (and fourth too) over other

games is flimsy. Never mind the lack of logic—playing for them makes you harder to beat.

PLAYING ONE STROKE AT A TIME—OR NOT?

Middle-grade players are told to think only of the stroke they are playing and lower-grade players are exhorted to do so. You should do the same thing only in lining up a winner or when hitting yourself out of trouble.

Other than that, such single concentration is over-engrossment. It hampers you, slows you down. As you play a shot that will come back you need to be thinking of that stroke and of your next position and stroke, actually three things at the same time. Appropriate combinations include:

- Serve and First Volley
- Deep First Volley and Moving In
- Approach Shot and Moving In
- Mark-Time Shot and Passing Shot
- Preparatory Drive to Forehand and Attack to Backhand
- Crosscourt Drive and Diagonal

Having your mind on your next shot does not lessen your chance of playing the present one properly; it increases it. When you can see you're going to receive an easy volley you *never* miss the approach shot. You don't miss the volley either, because your mind is ahead and waiting for the ball, making it seem slower.

Play a practice set and see how free you are if you allow yourself to think ahead. If your practice opponent is a weaker player, don't try for any winners at all and keep playing for the next shot. You will get a feeling of command not solely due to your being the stronger player.

REDUCING YOUR BALL-WATCHING LOAD

You do watch the ball—you're certainly not looking away at the cows in the corn—and probably you have your own special method of doing it, so that you won't forget. You watch it consciously, or for the whole of its flight, or particularly after the bounce, or until you can see its seams or its brand, or however else you believe is a fool-proof way.

Yet sooner or later you forget. You mis-hit badly and that reminds you to watch the ball. How long you haven't been watching it, goodness only knows.

It seems that it's beyond a player to watch the ball all the time—that is, without being obsessed with this and in consequence making his whole game slower.

Probably it's better to reduce your ball-watching load—to carry half of it well instead of all of it fairly poorly.

When you're not watching the ball you're looking ahead of it—meaning, you don't follow it beyond the last four feet or more in towards your racket—and you look ahead like that on the forehand side only. On the backhand side you watch the ball well, naturally. To make your stroke you place your right foot across and turn your right side around. And your head turns too and naturally drops towards and over the area of contact between ball and racket. This is the main reason why many players hit backhand volleys accurately and tape many forehand volleys.

On the forehand side you haven't the same natural tendency to drop your head towards the contact area. Watch any dozen players; in the warm-up they've got their heads down beautifully over every ball, but sooner or later in the set their heads are up on the forehand.

Focussing on the forehand side, you needn't worry about your smash, with left hand up and eyes glued to the ball, or about your serve, where you have the overriding principle of keeping your head up till you have hit the ball. Forehand groundstrokes and volleys (high, low and medium) are the offenders. As a short self-reminder, "Watch the ball on the forehand side."

TIMING

When playing a forehand drive no one would think of timing the ball with the flat loop of his combined backswing and forward-swing as one unit. No one times the ball from the *start* of his backswing, yet many players don't know exactly where their timing does begin. On a good day their timing comes naturally, but on a bad one they can't rectify it. What they regretfully know is that if they prepare too early their timing feels forced, and if too late it feels jerky.

Delay your timing. In your backswing, the racket head naturally goes farther back than your wrist, and in the forward swing it has to catch up with it—and so your racket head sweeps towards the ball faster than you'd imagine. Without having to hurry your forward swing, let alone snatch your racket forward, delay your timing to that fraction of time that exists between the end of your backswing and the beginning of your forward swing. Even though your racket is in motion, think of that fraction of change-over time as your timing pause. If you start your timing there it will be easiest.

Your timing pause is not a dead stop in your swing. It may be only a slight slowing down of your racket head. Against a fast ball it will be more mental than physical. But it's *there*. Sweep forward and time the ball from it. That's what you do, perhaps unknowingly, on a good day.

As for taking an early backswing, you take this comfortably early to give yourself a more comfortable timing pause, and that's all. Your backswing is not directly connected with your timing; to imagine it is only prolongs your timing and results in error. If you have time for a timing pause, even only a mental one, you have enough time to time the ball well.

Straight Backswing

If you play your forehand from a straight backswing, instead of with the more usual flat loop for momentum, your timing concept is the same. Swing back early and relatively slowly, pause for a fraction of a second (even if only mentally), and sweep forward with certainty. That is also how you play your backhand drive, since few people use a looped swing on that side.

In striving for the simplest timing, some players overdo their early preparation. They take the racket back very early and very quickly and then hold it there, stock still. Instead of the timing pause being a fraction of a second (but adequate), it lasts for seconds while they pose there. They've certainly got a clear timing pause to start from, but they're making too much of the timing part of their stroke, because after a dead stop they need a lot of effort to work up speed for their shot. Working away, some of these players drag their right shoulder forward and leave the racket head trailing behind; and this lack of coordination makes timing complicated instead of simple.

An excessive timing pause not only means hard work, but can lead to mistiming also.

Serving

Without bothering with a ball, wind up fully for a very hard low throw, *aimed*. You'll find that just before the forward movement you take a mental pause, for aim. That's the mental timing pause in your service. Your serve looks to be a continuous movement, but if this movement were all made at the same speed your swing would control you instead of you controlling it.

Contact

After you've timed a ball well it's a terrible waste to part with it too soon. Don't let it jump off the strings and go its own way. With a forehand drive, for example, hold it on the strings in long contact for a flat shot for depth, or hold it and roll it for a topspin crosscourt, or hold it with inside-underspin for a shot going away from your opponent's backhand.

It's like a catch. You have to hold onto the ball momentarily but distinctly, to complete the job your timing began.

Illus. 39. DELAY YOUR TIMING.
Because you never hit an "air shot"
with any other stroke, the smash
provides the clearest example of the
need to delay your timing to allow
for racket-head speed. You never
completely miss the ball AFTER it
has gone by.

Smashing

Take a long timing pause. A smash is practically all timing.
Unlike a forehand drive from the back of the court, a smash
contains power to burn in your sharply bent elbow—as Illus.
20 shows. (See Illus. 39 also.)

HANDLING CANNONBALL SERVES

It's maddening when you can't handle the erratic rocket
serving of an opponent who's really not much of a player at all.

His cannonballs land with fine impartiality either on the tape
or a foot out or just inside the diagonal corners—and the second

balls, if they're not double faults, have plenty of speed too. You're forced into missing or giving him very easy volleys, and in one way or another he's cracking in enough fast balls to hold his service games. Any moment he'll string together a fluke and a net cord and a liner or bad bounce and he'll break one of yours.

In the left court you're playing the ball as a backhand volley and holding your own, but in the right your short forehands aren't strong enough as cuts or blocks and he's making you look bad, even battered. You know the shot you want: a short-backswing forehand coming over and round the ball, but no matter how fast you get your racket back you just *cannot* time it.

What has gone wrong is this. When you whip your racket back for a short straight backswing, your wrist makes the short swing that is in your mind but the momentum of the fast racket head (weight $\times$ *speed*) swings it farther back than you imagine. So, you are mistiming. The faster you take your racket back to give yourself fractionally more time, the farther back the head hinges from your wrist and you continue to mistime the ball.

The remedy cannot be to take your backswing more slowly (because against rockets that's only wishful thinking), and it is not to stiffen your wrist to keep that wayward racket head strictly in line with your forearm. A stiff wrist and probably a grip of iron too is no good for covering unpredictable cannonballs, which always accentuate any bad bounce.

What you have to do is take your wrist back a shorter distance. (If you always see your own strokes in relation to your racket face rather than in relation to your wrist, feel that the face is more handily-close than before.)

Play cannonballs with a free wrist and with strong palm and fingers, since this is far quicker and more flexible than playing with a ramrod arm. Take your wrist back very little and the racket-head backswing will be long enough. Then swing forward and hit over and around the ball—and the shot should be yours. If, before swinging forward, you've had time for that fractional mental timing pause, the shot *will* be yours.

Do not see this shot as a mere wrist flick. It is a very short-backswing forehand made by a free but strongly-controlled wrist.

If your shot tends to go high you are standing up too straight, knocked back on your heels somewhat by speed. Lean forward more than usual. For footwork, see Illus. 40.

On seeing an older player handle cannonball serves, onlookers credit him with wonderful eyesight and amazing reflexes, or perhaps with a marvellous memory for the days of his youth. Perhaps you too once wondered how he did it.

SALVAGING YOUR GAME ON BAD DAYS

On their good days, experienced and inexperienced players are alike. From the moment they step on the court everything feels right and the ball almost seems to be working for them.

They see the ball clearly and send it, with little effort, sailing well over the net at good speed, curving into a safe downward path. There's plenty of time for their timing pause and long contact on every stroke. Feet? They don't even notice that they own any.

On bad days experienced and inexperienced players part company. The former mend their games, the latter play badly all day.

It does not take years of match play to be able to salvage your game on a bad day.

Warm-Up

There's no time to waste. If your forehand has an unwanted slice in it and your backhand flies high, go straight up to the net and play a few sharp volleys and then go back to the baseline and start as a new man.

Even if you feel bleary-eyed in an early morning match and are guiltily certain that's the trouble after a late night, the real trouble is your feet—the very foot movements you scarcely

Illus. 40. RIGHT-FOOT COVER. Against fast wide serving don't try to get your left foot across first if you find you're always being caught in mid-jump. Your weight is then going sideways and is not only wasted but interferes with your timing. Instead, get your right foot down first and play along your front (left) leg.

notice on a good day. Move your feet quickly, and your eyesight will look after itself.

You can't expect miracles in a short warm-up, so be prepared to battle along after the set begins.

Isolate Your Trouble

An inexperienced player thinks his whole game is off, and sure enough his better strokes decline to the level of his bad ones. When an experienced player's backhand is off, he resolutely does not let that affect his service.

Most of the time you can only play as well as your opponent allows you to, so on an off-day it is hard to reach your good form against a capable opponent who is normally too strong for you anyway. More often, though, your good form is just around the corner. You have already experienced this, probably without noticing it, in a practice game. Bad game, bad conditions, weak opponent, and you, with little interest, are scarcely better. Then suddenly you happen to hit one type of shot perfectly, and do it again. You have found your interest, and everything falls into place. It has happened to everybody.

Keys

When you play well, note why. Go further if you like, and when practicing notice how you *don't* like to hit the ball (such as from weak dead feet, or cramped hunched shoulder, or spraying to the off side, or too high), and then note the correction or key that makes it exactly right.

Your keys will be yours, they're personal. Here are some.

Footwork. Your feet are like a receptacle. Bleary eyes and everything else go to your feet—tiredness, lack of interest, nervousness, and even a sore arm. Make your feet a strong pivot instead. It's said that a certain player is only as good as his serve, but (better) every player is only as good as his feet.

Past the Net. Hit every ball past the net. Range from there.

Ball. Watch it on the stroke that you're playing worst.

Serve. High and low—keep your head up and your back toe on the ground. Middle—reduce your action, but don't stint on elbow-bending.

Forehand. Lean forward. Check timing pause and long contact. Against fast balls, short backswing with wrist or racket head.

Backhand. Turn well across to your left. Plant your right foot strongly before hitting the ball.

Topspin. Roll the ball along the short strings and *make* it spin.

Volley. Volley in front, so you can see the ball. Forehand volley—if you don't keep your wrist low, the racket face may be more open (tilted upwards) than you think. In lowering your wrist you tend to roll it forward a little at the same time, closing the face a little—and that's the way you usually volley and that's the racket face angle you always imagine you have.

Lob. If you lob short, hit flat instead of with underspin. Hit the second one out rather than short again, and range from there.

Smash. Put left hand up for balance and keep right elbow well bent. Hit the ball in front of you but aim well above the net.

Remedying your strokes will not exasperate you if they genuinely interest you. They must, or you'd never have persevered to become a good player.

MINOR MISFORTUNES

When your opponent begins the match with a slight physical handicap or some minor misfortune befalls him later, you don't expect him to lose the match through it. But how different it feels when it happens to you.

If you begin your game with a stiff finger joint spoiling your grip or a ricked neck hampering your movement, these things are at their worst early. They interfere less and less as you get warmed up and absorbed. They may be worse tomorrow, but then it's too late.

If you fall heavily don't continue straight on and lose points while you wonder where you have grazed or cut yourself. And don't let any blood from your fingers ooze onto the handle and put you off. Get up and go straight over to the water tap at the side of the court. Wash, dry, use sticking plaster. (Keep it in your pocket, along with the folding money you don't leave behind in the dressing room either.) See how your grip feels with the sticking plaster on, and go back and pick up the game where you left off, that is, ready to win the next point.

On the other hand, if you twist your ankle or knee or crash your hip against a fence post, don't go off to the side of the court—limping and feeling worse with every painful step. Stay where you are and rub it so hard that you can't feel anything else, and then play on and keep moving. Next week the doctor will say you were foolish, but that's only a medical opinion.

You have a frayed center string almost breaking, and no second racket, and sure enough at 3-all in the third set it does break, and one or two strings on either side sag badly. The racket's finished, so you borrow one. Despite hope, a borrowed racket never feels the same. Use the few moments you have at courtside to get on terms with its grip and balance (discount the weight). Do that instead of feeling sorry for yourself because the racket's not identical.

Grip larger; all right. But more oblong; O.K. When the balance is head-heavy swing the racket about in simulated serve and drive, holding it at the extreme end of the handle in thumb and three fingers and making it feel as head-heavy as a sledge hammer; then take your normal grip. If handle-heavy, swing it with a short grip to make the head feel as ineffectual as a ping-pong paddle; then take your normal grip. It's all over in a minute.

Win the match and get a pat on the back from your opponent and friends. If you pick up your broken racket and feel that *it* is a bit strange, take another pat on the back—from yourself.

GAMESMANSHIP

Once this meant, "How to beat your friends without actually cheating." It was confined to social play mostly, applied as straight-faced humor.

Long since, it has come to mean everything that can put your opponent off his game, from discourtesy all the way to calling a ball incorrectly. So it can be a soft word for cheating.

Don't indulge in gamesmanship.

Using it belittles you. Even if a man is a powerful player or if his game is beautifully crisp or smooth, if he's a gamesman, that's what he mainly becomes known as.

Combatting It

When your opponent calls a ball out that was in, be determined to get your next shot in. And the next. Instead of putting you off, let him put you "on."

Your opponent is the one who has to think up his gamesmanship act and stage it and recover from it and then play on again. If he doesn't succeed in upsetting you, he will be distracted, not you. Starting from a position of looking down on gamesmen, about the only thing you need is patience, and you won't need that for very long either. In all instances be more ready to play the next point than he is. When you combat gamesmanship this way, it looks futile.

Arriving Late

This is supposed to make you nervous, waiting about on tenterhooks. But he only gets ten or fifteen minutes' grace by the rules, and he can't arrive when the score is at match point or even the vital seventh. You're only waiting for the warm-up. Take the edge off your game? Probably you could do with a little less edge.

Be completely ready to go on court though. Don't have him rushing up at the last minute, but ready, making *you* hurry with some last minute thing.

Possibly in the warm-up he'll hit about two balls and then say it's late and he's ready when you are. Say, "Can't worry about that now," and go through your routine warm-up.

A great aid to patience and calmness and feeling normal is to know that once you are on the court it is not *late*; it is only *now*, as always.

Stalling

Another gamesman may waste time at every change-over, which leaves you waiting out on court.

Is that so terrible? It's better to be there first. You're *ready*.
Another dawdles between points. Let him, and let his mind
wander more than yours while he's doing it. Pity he doesn't
take longer.

Another lags between some points and hurries starting others.
No opponent is a metronome and the difference is only seconds.
Be ready always.

One serves a fast first ball and follows right in, but it's a
fault—and then he takes forever going back, and even looks
across at the matches on either side . . . and at long last, his
second serve comes over. Would you like to serve with a long
break like that between your serves?

You've won a succession of games and feel in the groove. To
break your streak, he says he must get his knee-band and runs
off to the dressing room. You're left on the court. What of it?
It's he, not you, who has to hurry away, go into the shade and
come out again into the sun, put the thing on, pick up his
racket, start again. Never mind any streak, you're better prepared than he is to win the next point, especially when you
know how to play the first point after any break. You play it
as a point late in the game, with soundest tactical shots.

Like arriving late, stalling needn't put you off in the least.

Brow-Beating

You call a very close ball Out (which it is, or you wouldn't
have called it) and he tries to belittle you. He may be cold—
"Has the ball got to be a foot in?" Or dramatic—arms raised
to the spectators. Or violent—"What!?" with racket flung on
court and hands jammed on hips.

Take up your position to serve or receive. Call the next
similar ball Out too.

He's a net-game player and you have to be very quick in
returning his fast services. One just misses and you call "Fault"
as you return it—and he tells you not to hit faults back. Say,
"Only the close ones," and stick to it.

The Whole Gamut

As long as gamesmanship continues there will be new ploys. You may be nervous and keen but as long as you're not impatient it's hard to see how any tricks can distract or upset you more than they do the perpetrator. No incident can go on forever—it has to end quickly if you don't take part in it—and once on court you've got plenty of time.

Irritating Habits

Don't be touchy and look for gamesmanship where none exists, and distract yourself looking for it. A player may bounce the ball many times and then stand up to serve (and you're all ready)—but then he goes back for two more quick bounces, then ups and serves (and you're not ready).

The first time it happens you can hardly believe your eyes, but when he repeats his performance you know it's his habit. Don't let this crazy serve irritate you, game after game. Just be thankful it isn't yours.

Non-Enemy

A strange thing is that if you always act in this way, gamesmen will come to like you. Perhaps they've found you hard to beat and respect you for it or perhaps you're just one of their few non-enemies. They give up gamesmanship against you in future, and perhaps they will give it up altogether. Perhaps you've helped to save a soul from sin.

And it doesn't matter how young you are.

7. YOUR OWN NET-GAME DOUBLES

Responsibility is shared in doubles and the play is short and fast, so your match temperament is usually good. However, when playing with a stronger partner, avoid self-consciousness. He can't help you when you're hitting the ball, so play determinedly from start to finish. Self-effacement slows your movement, weakens your play, and doesn't help him. If you must say "sorry," say it only now and then in politeness and never in abject sorrow.

For a pair to combine well is a great asset, but whether you're playing with a new or a regular partner your own *play* is always the main thing.

Whether your partner is stronger, weaker or about equal, play by two principles. One, play as few groundstrokes as possible (none at all when you're server or net man if you can help it). Two, cover your side of the court *from net to baseline*. These two principles of play are also the basis of the combination of any pair playing net-game doubles, in which both players strongly seek a net barrier and are hard, or impossible, to lob over.

YOUR SERVICE GAMES

This sequence is your aim: serve—move in—first volley—move in to form a net barrier with your partner. This will give you a dominating position, even though you may be playing a good pair who return your serves well.

The consistency of your first serves is more important than the speed of some of them—because your first volley is nearly always more aggressively played after a first serve than a second, and mostly your first volley decides the ultimate fate of the point.

Serve deeply, so that the receiver's return has farther to travel and allows you to move in closer for your first volley. Serve to your opponent's slower side, even if it's the steadier. This is normally the backhand, but if he cuts his forehand and rolls his backhand, serve to his forehand. Play the points; pick up an early one against a fast erratic forehand here and there, but on the later ones mainly keep away from the most potentially dangerous stroke any receiver has.

Since few of your serves are aces and most do not force a weak return, you can remain in better balance and be more effective if you regard your serve as being a strong approach shot for your first volley.

With your partner assisting, you have less court to cover than in net-game singles, so for your doubles first volley move in faster and closer. Play your first volley from *inside* the service line. Whatever type of service you use, recognize and use its advantage for moving well in; if it's topspin, its high arc gives you time; if it's sliced, your right leg comes straight through and gives you a flying start.

If your first volley is not difficult, take charge, mostly by playing it deep. If it's very difficult, scramble hard. Serve and move in with the determination of never missing it.

Playing a weaker pair and leading in games, carelessness in your serving games is most likely to occur in one of three places: your first serve, your first volley, and in points to the left court when you are a point ahead or at 40-love.

Danger Court

Against the normal evenly-balanced pair of right-handers, the danger court is not the left court, even though all game points against you except 15-40 are played from that side. The points there are easier to hold, on some practical counts:

● Your serve to the backhand corner is a long diagonal, so you can get more first balls in

● The receiver returns with his backhand

- The receiver's net-man partner has his backhand towards the center and his interceptions are not as threatening
- Your first volley can be played uninterruptedly to the receiver's backhand
- If the receiver lobs, his lob can be covered by a forehand overhead from either your net partner or yourself.

The right is the danger court:

- It's more difficult for you to land your serve on the receiver's backhand
- Most fast topspin forehand drives are hit from the right court (especially against your second serve), and most interceptions are made by the right-court receiver's net man
- Playing your first volley clear of this opposing net man mostly sends it back to the receiver's forehand
- Lobbing from his forehand, a right-court receiver can force your net partner to use only his backhand overhead—and if, as server, you ever have to cover such a lob yourself, it has to be done with your backhand.

To stifle this right-court danger you need to be able to serve down the center at will, with first and second balls alike. If your serve is sliced it's difficult to do that, at will. Bear in mind that a dangerous right-court receiver is always trying to make a fast attacking topspin forehand of everything, to give you such an awkward first volley or half volley that his net man will intercept it. See Illus. 11 again.

However, let's say you're keeping to your sliced serve, because your wide serving is strong and day in day out the sliced serve is undoubtedly your best serve. To find your opponent's backhand in the right court it's probably best to vary your position between center-mark and sideline—because each position offers its own chance of success, but none is without its drawback if you keep to it all the time. See Illus. 41.

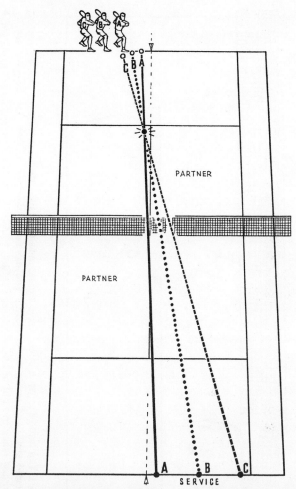

Illus. 41. SLICED SERVE TO RIGHT-COURT RECEIVER'S BACKHAND.
A–A: Stand near center mark and serve down receiver's center line. If you do that all the time the receiver comes to welcome this serve and the open court it leaves.
B–B: Your position forces him to stand wider. But can you continuously serve over the wrong side of the net-band without straying too far either right or left? To the right's a forehand, to the left a fault.
C–C: Your threatened wide ace makes him uncover a fair amount of backhand space. But familiarity breeds contempt—the combined angle and curve of your serve do make it easy to step around.

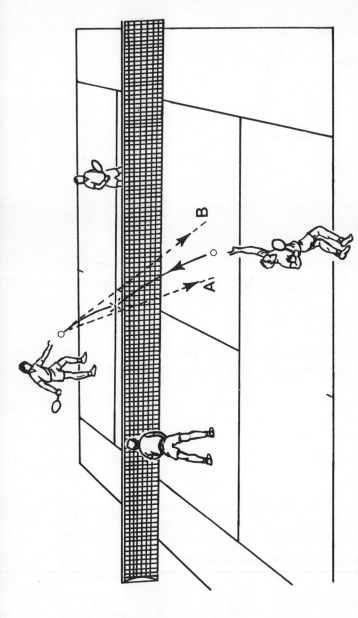

Illus. 42. IDEAL POSITION. You curve a topspin-sliced serve almost automatically into the receiver's body, preventing him from making a forceful shot, and in the same motion you advance inside the service line. Pause there for volleying balance and widest reach to right or left: Receiver's return, to A or B, avoids the net man but gives you a comfortable first volley to play deeply from backhand or forehand. Close in and form your net barrier for a perfect position. You have done all the play so far, but in combination your partner is watchful for a lob attempted either over his head or down the middle (towards your backhand overhead).

Illus. 43. LINE UP WITH LINE OF FLIGHT. Most players work on the whole of the ball's flight and line up with the spot where they want the ball to land. Some feel that the latter part of the ball's curve takes it more to the left than aimed, especially when serving from out near the sideline; they line up with the ball's early line of flight, in effect a shade more sideways. Use whichever method gives you more confidence in your aim.

Finding the right-court receiver's backhand is simpler with a topspin or topspin-sliced serve—much more automatic. Instead of being under pressure yourself you're free to concentrate on jamming his backhand, and then the right court is a danger court no longer. For an ideal position, see Illus. 42.

You need accuracy, and since many things in tennis begin with your feet it helps if you line them up well. See Illus. 43.

Regarding strokes deciding match temperament or the other way about, recall a position you must surely have experienced before: Your serve, deciding set, 4-5 down, 30-all, first serve a fault and aggressive receiver poised. Your match temperament and likely success depend less on any "iron nerve" than on whether your serve feels like Illus. 41 or like Illus. 42.

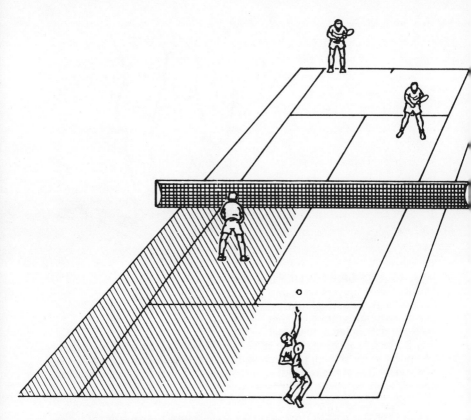

Illus. 44. NET MAN'S COVER. You can't do it by standing close to the net, playing only easy volleys and leaving the center (to say nothing of lobs) to your partner. Stand halfway between net and service line and almost halfway between sideline and centerline, and don't over-protect your seldom-attacked sideline. It's easier for you to volley than for your partner. Be a lively netman, the type you don't like receiving against.

AS NET MAN

It's your duty to cover your side of the court from net to baseline. As well as that, protect your more vulnerable moving-in partner as much as possible so that he is more free to cover his outside sidelines against dangerous short crosscourt returns. You've a lot to cover. See Illus. 44.

Play that way, also, when your partner's the strong man. As a pair, you're more likely to lose if you're Never There than if you miss a few shots. Get rid of any idea that your serving partner, stronger or equal, is 99 per cent responsible for winning his serves, your contribution merely amounting to standing in front of your sideline and smashing a short lob and making a wide interception now and then. All net-game net men have better intentions than that, but sometimes it's all many of them actually do.

Lobs

The worst thing you can do is get lobbed over.

It's not so bad if you let a drive slip through the center, because your partner is somewhere in line with the shot and can usually volley it in some fashion himself. But he can't be prepared to alter course for a lob and get inside the service line for his first volley, both at the same time. You chase the lob, of course, and probably retrieve it, but the damage has almost certainly been done.

Take 10 marks for alertly covering a lob; 6 or 7 for a desperation cover (Illus. 19); 1 for retrieving a lob; and 0 for not.

AS RECEIVER'S NET MAN
Strong Partner

When playing with a partner who has a strong service return (hard, low, dipping, and always clear of the net man), you should try to have a field day at the net against the troubled server's succession of upward first volleys and half volleys. Don't limit your opportunities by standing too near the sideline or too close to the net.

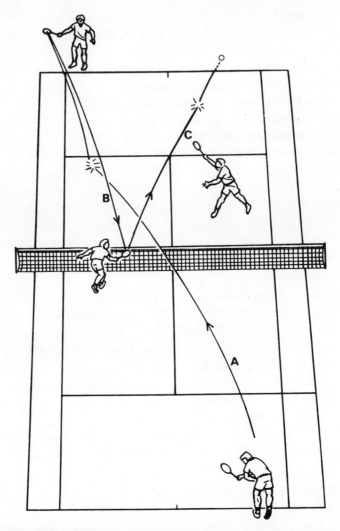

Illus. 45. THREE PENALTIES. You're out of the game, the opposing net man has a field day, and your partner becomes either disappointed with his own game or most annoyed with your tactics.

Stand at least halfway between the singles sideline and the center line for wide coverage and no closer than halfway between net and service line to give yourself time for this coverage. Reach well forward to volley the ball closer to the net whenever the chance comes.

You can take up this position while the server is serving or you can begin by standing at your service line. Some players like to be stationed in the same manner as when their partner is serving, and others prefer to see their receiving partner hit the ball and then to move in with it.

Strong, But Erratic

Take up the same position.

About Average

Most receivers have fair success in attacking the first serve and better results in attacking the second. Stand at about your service line and see the ball being hit, moving in if the going's good.

If the server's first serves are too good for your partner, stay back beside him, to give both of you a better chance of continuing the point. Go up for the second balls.

Whenever your partner asks you to stay back, do so at once.

Weak Service Return

Your partner may have a strong serve-and-volley game but be weak on service return. Stay back.

When you're the strongest player on the court and your partner the weakest, it's stupid to take a net position. You're inviting the opposing net man to play the game of his life. (See Illus. 45.)

Toss-Volleys

Returning to the usual game of four about-equal players, your correct net position does not invite the server to play his

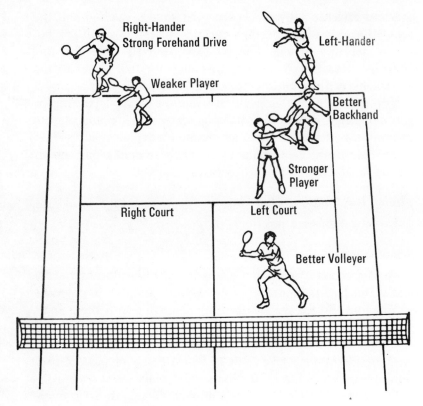

Right-Hander
Strong Forehand Drive

Left-Hander

Weaker Player

Better
Backhand

Stronger
Player

Right Court

Left Court

Better Volleyer

Illus. 46. RIGHT OR LEFT COURT.

first volley as a toss-volley over your head. You're therefore free to cover the center.

It is dangerous for the server to play a low first volley as a toss-volley, since it is often within your smashing reach before it gains its full height, and when he gets a higher ball he al-most always prefers a more direct shot.

However, if your one idea is to stand very close to the net in the left court and crash winners from leaping forehand inter-ceptions, the server can play forehand toss-volleys over your backhand overhead side with comparative ease.

AS RECEIVER

A general guide to courts is in Illus. 46.

Attack

Just as you must attack against a net-game singles player, always attack against a net-game doubles pair. If you have a strong topspin drive and their serves are moderate, make it a full-scale attack. If their serves are strong and you play a cool and steady game of low service returns at varying pace mixed with a few lobs on occasion, regard your game as a counterattack.

Adopting a defensive outlook merely because you're receiving leads to tentative play. Such play relies on your opponents' mistakes; they may make some early, but you play them into form for the later and more important stage of the match. You should always play the ball, but defensive thought often results in the ball playing you—and it also makes you slow to take unexpected opportunities.

The Battle for the Net

Against a good pair you need to handle fast serves well so that you don't let the net man intercept and you don't continually give the server comfortable first volleys. You try to prevent the server from forming a net barrier. You form a receiver's net barrier at every opportunity.

Fast Serves

Play as previously described under Cannonballs: short-backswing forehand, and backhand as for a volley. From the left court you have time to do more with your backhand and should roll it—because a doubles server gets closer to the net for his first volley than a net-game singles player can.

With forehands in the right court and backhands in left, hitting outside and over the ball keeps it clear of the net·man and should give the server a low first volley.

Whether a serve is fast or only moderate, rising-ball service

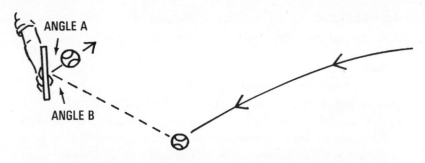

ANGLE A

ANGLE B

Illus. 47. RISING-BALL REBOUND. Rebound angle A, theoretically equal to contact angle B, is sharply upwards. It's more sharply upwards when the received ball has topspin on it. However, a relatively small racket-face closure takes care of things. Don't rush or jerk just because it's a rising ball; try to play a perfect stroke.

returns are the most effective. Rising-ball shots tend to fly out of control, so to have confidence in them consciously play outside and over the ball with a closed racket face. "Closed round the ball" was discussed on page 46, referring to wide forehand volleys; for the necessity of "closing over the ball" see Illus. 47.

Preventing Their Net Barrier

As soon as the server puts his first volley safely into play he moves up beside his partner and forms their net barrier—from where they win most of the points, and yet another service is held. Only your service return can prevent them from forming their net barrier in the first place.

A good pair normally play as shown in Illus. 42 and box you up, but they can't keep to the straight and narrow path all through a match. Take your opportunities of preventing a net barrier whenever they occur, even though infrequently. (See Illus. 48.)

Although the server won't serve many AD balls, your usual forehand service return tries to have a similar effect to DE, that is, to give your net man a good chance to intercept.

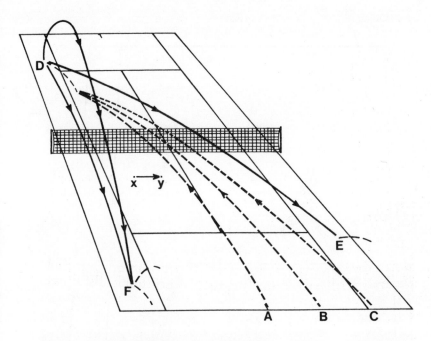

Illus. 48. PREVENTING THEIR NET BARRIER.

A–D–E: Server intends surprising you with a wide ball—which doesn't work. You hit it at D, playing your rising-ball forehand wide towards E for a possible winner or a probable interception by your partner if the server scrambles it back.

B–D–F: Serve is short and net man tries to protect the center, but too early, before you're committed to your direction. Push your wrist forward and play a simple passing shot DF.

C–D–F: Here the serve has not been directed to your exposed backhand side, nor has it forced you uncomfortably wide. It's short and slow and the net man thinks you'll hit it hard—and he's unprepared for your lob over his backhand side.

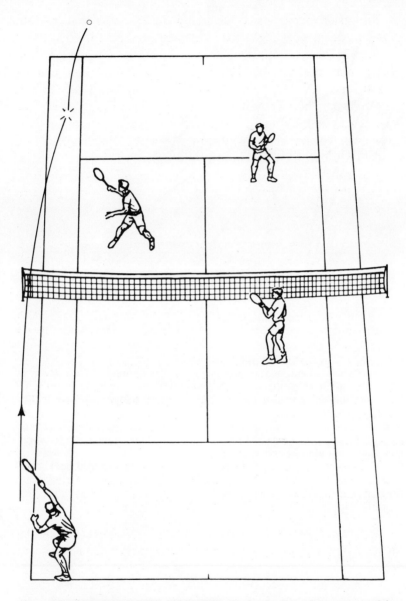

Illus. 49. SERVICE RETURN SIDELINER. Perfectly done, but opportunities for safely winning down the sideline are few. Do not over-indulge.

Your sideliner is less often easily presented to you, as DF, than made in more demanding fashion, as shown in Illus. 49.

As for lobs, DF (as a lob) is a shot you shouldn't forget. Many players think of a lob as being made in defense against a fast serve—but that's where the speed and the extra effect of any irregular bounce make it difficult to be sure of hitting the center of your strings. Serving, these players think a slower serve will always be hit hard, and are less prepared for a lob, which you can hit with certainty. Keep it in mind.

The same players' outlook is that lobs are more likely to come from the left-court receiver's backhand than from anywhere else. Such lobs, however, are not effective, since they can be covered by either of the serving players with his forehand overhead. A lob is more dangerous when you play it from wide in the right court, over the net man's backhand overhead. Keep that in mind too.

A successful lob prevents the serving pair from forming their net barrier, in only one hit. Use it consistently if you're allowed to, and even when you're against a generally alert net man don't put it completely out of your mind.

Mostly, however, you can't prevent the server from making his net barrier. Opportunities for successful sideliners and lobs are few and your service returns are usually volleyed safely into play by the incoming server's first volley.

Receivers' Net Barrier

At the same time as you're trying to prevent the server forming his net barrier, try to form your own receivers' barrier. Receiving does not mean being automatically relegated to a One Up One Back formation.

If the net man has to retrieve one of your lobs, go up. If he's going to cover it, barely, with an off-balance backhand overhead, go up.

If you can force the net man into making a defensive volley that you can attack strongly, follow in after this attacking shot. (See Illus. 50 on next page.)

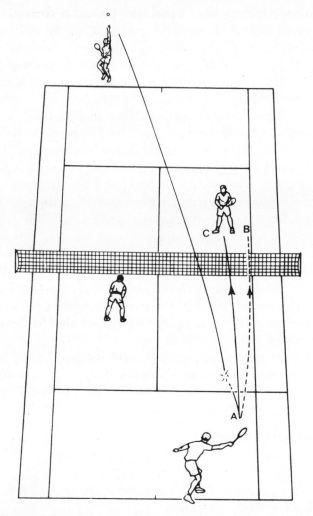

Illus. 50. ATTACKING THE NET MAN. It's often easier to attack the net man than to sideline him. Never play AB, giving him a swiftly-made crosscourt backhand volley winner. Attack his right hip. If his volley is defensive and short, attack low and down the center of your opponent's barrier and follow your shot in. All four players are then at the net.

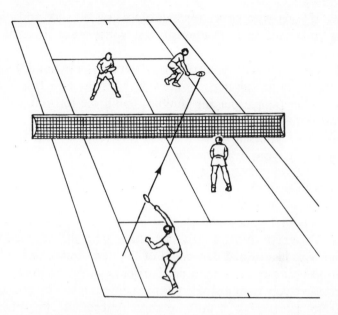

Illus. 51. NET-BARRIER DUEL. You can't stop the server from getting his serve in, and advancing to play his first volley, and then moving in closer to form his net barrier. And you can't follow your return in if it's high, or if you're not in balance to follow straight in along with the ball, or even if you've played from too far back to have time to move well in before you volley. But if you're a truly net-conscious player, his serve will have to be severe before it will prevent you from forming a receivers' net barrier. It's from two net barriers that exciting rapid-fire volleying exchanges are played.

Mostly, you form your receivers' net barrier from your service return to the incoming server's first volley. It has to be a good shot, but you can do it. Get behind a rising ball; with your weight going forward in perfect balance, hit the ball low across the net with either topspin dip or glided slice and move in to volley the server's upward first volley. (See Illus. 51 on previous page.)

It's positive to have your receivers' net barrier in mind. Everyone imagines he's going to follow in when he can, but if you watch other people playing doubles you'll see for yourself the opportunities that go begging.

Try to set yourself up to move in on every serve. If the first ball prevents you, dwell on the second.

When You're Back

When you haven't been able to go in and the server has played his first volley and formed his net barrier, you're then in a similar position to the baseliner playing an all-court player who has gained command of the net. You're in a worse position because a two-man net barrier covers a doubles court more effectively than a single net man covers a singles court.

Again, never play a nothing shot. Attack, in one form or another. If the server's first volley is short, go for a winner while you have the chance. If his volley is back at your feet go for the "half-drive," and if his shot ties you up awkwardly try to hit yourself out of trouble. If a lob seems all that's left to play, hit it high and give your partner time to come back and join you.

Often the server's first volley is what could be called average. From this you play very low over the center strap so that he will have to play a low volley and give you another chance. Your intention is to draw him close to the net to make this volley and your hope is that he will linger there, so that your next shot can be a lob safely over his head—where you'll either have a winner or you'll be in to form that coveted receivers' net barrier.

Misplaced Advice

"Just put the ball back and let him make the mistakes," is good advice for a singles match against an erratic baseliner.

In net-game receiving it amounts to providing the server with a succession of comfortable first volleys, and no doubt the net man with more than his usual share of interceptions. Set your sights higher than that and play with a clear conscience.

LEFT-HANDED RECEIVER

If you're a left-hander with great strength in your topspin forehand (or a right-hander with a similar two-handed backhand) you should always play your doubles from the left court. Service returns are paramount, not subsequent shots you make from the center of the court.

Tandem

If your left-handed forehand is dominating the game, expect your opponents to play tandem against you. The server serves from beside the center-mark, from where he can't fail to find your backhand, and shuts your forehand out of the game. He can't do that with the orthodox formation without exposing almost all of his backhand court, so he plays tandem. And if this formation unsettles you, he wins the points without trouble.

Instead, regard tandem as a weak tactic: *there is no net man standing opposite you.*

Incorrect Tandem

Desperate to shut out your winning forehand, your opponents may play tandem against you on the spur of the moment without one of them knowing much about it. If it's the net man, his incorrect net position allows you to play over him or past him. If it's the server he's slow in covering his unaccustomed side of the court. (See Illus. 52 on next page.)

When tandem is not well played against you and the server goes further and misses his first ball, your backhand becomes very much the attacker instead of being the attacked.

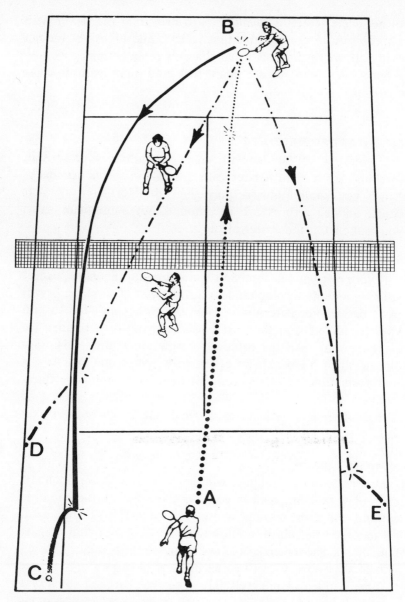

Illus. 52. (see opposite page).

Well-Played Tandem

Sooner or later you'll have to face well-played tandem, where BE is the only shot available to you. Your inside-underspin shot giving the swiftly-advancing server a comfortable first volley, won't do.

To make anything of BE you have to develop a downward outside slice, played from the top of the service bounce or on the rise. Turn well sideways, hold your wrist low . . . etc. See Illus. 16 again, where the shot is shown as a backhand volley.

Follow it in whenever you can. You have the advantage of playing it into a space where no net man stands; don't let the server have the same empty-space advantage with *his* first volley if there's any chance of your being able to move in.

Against that sort of play your opponents call off their tandem. You may even be sorry to see it go.

Illus. 52. (opposite page) LEFT-HANDER UPSETTING TANDEM.

AGAINST NET MAN. If you see him standing close to the center to guard it, lob over his backhand side, BC. Next time he'll stand farther back to prevent this and you can see BD as an opening for your low inside-underspin backhand.

AGAINST SERVER. Play BE. It's not one of your stronger shots, but play it calmly; the server needs to get well over to his right and probably won't volley from inside the service line.

Tandem is an uncomfortable formation to operate. If both players try to guard their sidelines, the net man leaves the center open and the server moves away from it.

APPENDIX 1

GRIPS AND STYLES

A player's style is basically named from his forehand grip.

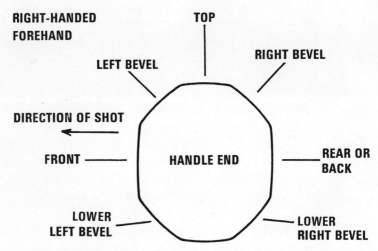

RIGHT-HANDED FOREHAND

TOP

LEFT BEVEL

RIGHT BEVEL

DIRECTION OF SHOT

FRONT —— HANDLE END —— REAR OR BACK

LOWER LEFT BEVEL

LOWER RIGHT BEVEL

Illus. 53. HANDLE SURFACES. Racket face is square to the net.

FOREHAND

Handle Surfaces
See Illus. 53.

Grip Classifications
For a diagrammatic presentation by thumb and forefinger V position, see Illus. 54–58. Five names are used, whereas once the Australian and Extreme-Eastern grips were either included in Eastern or were called in-betweens.

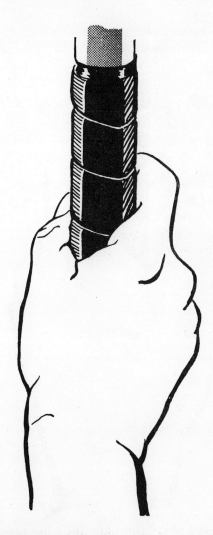

Illus. 54. CONTINENTAL FOREHAND GRIP. The thumb and forefinger V lies somewhere on the left bevel.

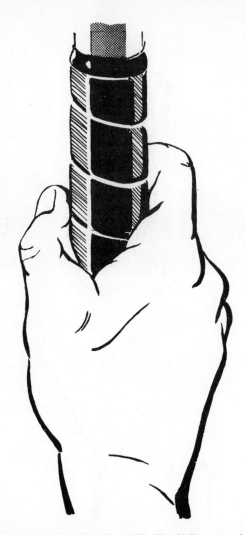

Illus. 55. AUSTRALIAN FOREHAND GRIP. The V lies anywhere between the left bevel and just left of the center of the top surface.

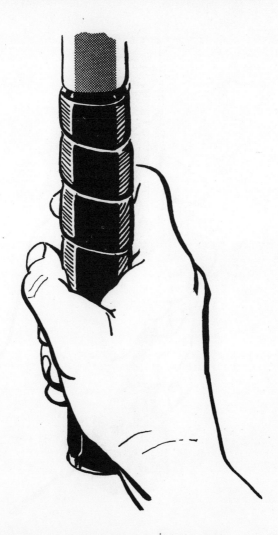

Illus. 56. EASTERN FOREHAND GRIP. The V lies anywhere from the center of the top surface to the right edge of the top surface.

Illus. 57. EXTREME-EASTERN FOREHAND GRIP. The V lies somewhere on the right bevel. This grip is also used in the Semi-Western style, where the forehand is looped and more related to the Western style than to the Eastern.

Illus. 58. WESTERN FOREHAND GRIP. The V lies anywhere from the right edge of the right bevel to the rear surface.

THUMB AND FOREFINGER V. The V position gives the clearest diagram, but note that Illus. 54–58 conveniently use the same relatively sized hands and handles and in Illus. 54–57 show a similar manner of holding the racket, namely, handle diagonally across the palm with forefinger extended. Your hand may be larger or smaller in relation to the handle, or you may use a grip with your fingers more closed. Since either of these differences slightly alters the V position, this method of comparison may not provide a positive grip identification. Nor does anyone ever *feel* the V position of his grip when he hits the ball.

HEEL OF HAND. Here it can be fairly precisely said: Heel on top, Continental; heel on right bevel, Australian; on rear surface, Eastern to Extreme-Eastern; on lower right bevel, Western. For most players this corresponds with their V positions. One point it does clearly settle is that although a bunched-finger grip may bring the V very near to the center of the top surface, if the heel of the hand lies on the right bevel the grip is Australian and not Eastern.

Only a Continental player feels the heel of his hand much, and then mainly as a non-twisting feeling of strength of grip. When hitting the ball, feel comes from farther along your hand.

PALM. This provides the best grip-feel, very small changes in your palm position giving you a distinctly different feeling between one grip and the next. Palm above top surface, Continental; palm towards the top, Australian; solidly behind racket handle, Eastern; farther behind again, Extreme-Eastern; and palm mainly under the handle, Western.

When driving the ball, the main feel comes from your palm and the lower part of your index finger.

BASE KNUCKLE OF INDEX FINGER. In the five grips this knuckle moves from the right bevel around to the lower right bevel, but this is more an adjunct to your grip than a basis. Its position is of consequence only in the Eastern and Extreme-

Eastern grips, where it lies behind the rear surface and is strongly felt in the stroke.

WRIST. Wrist is not a satisfactory means of grip-identification, wrist above handle applying to both Continental and Australian and wrist behind handle to all of the remaining three. "Wrist" is less associated with grip-position than with the manner of using it, such as freely, firmly or loosely, or holding it low for volleying.

FINGERTIPS. Position of the fingertips in any grip is greatly affected by the length of a player's fingers and can thus be an imprecise means of identification. For the average hand-to-grip relation, however, Illus. 56 and 57 show a noticeable difference in position for the Eastern and Extreme-Eastern grips. Also you can tell the difference between a Continental and an Australian grip by whether the ends of your fingers feel that they are resting mainly on the lower left bevel or a little up the flatter front surface of the handle.

When driving the ball, fingertips are mostly tighteners, but for touch shots and volleys there's a lot of feel in the whole length of your fingers.

Associations

Continental and Australian are associated. Both have palm positions toward the top and easy access to the backhand.

Eastern and Extreme-Eastern are a pair, having strong forward forehands and a large change of grip for an adequate backhand.

Extreme-Eastern and Semi-Western have the same grip but yet are not a pair because of their different styles. The Extreme-Eastern swings forward and the Semi-Western more up-and-over.

Semi-Western and Western are a close pair.

Altering Your Grip

Since your forehand is your most individual shot it is usually better to improve it by some means other than altering your grip. Two vital aspects of your forehand are the spot where your racket meets the ball in relation to your body and the angle of your racket face at contact—and with your existing grip you're used to these. If, for example, you alter from Continental to Eastern to have more power, you need to meet the ball farther in front of your body. You can determinedly do that, but many a player who has altered his forehand grip is left with a hesitancy in timing the ball, noticeably favoring dropping-ball play for medium balls and being all at sea in timing an unexpectedly fast one. His natural timing ability has gone—but not forever, because it returns as soon as he tries his original grip once more.

As for the angle of your racket face at contact, with your original grip you can swing your racket with your eyes shut and know it's square to the net, but if you alter from Eastern to Continental for more flexibility it will be slightly more open (tilted upwards). In theory, meeting the ball not so far in front of your body should also give you a square contact, so you should kill two birds with one stone, but in practice you're always fighting to keep the ball lower than it seems to want to go.

Altering from Continental to Eastern makes your forehand stronger, but it feels more clumsy and you have less touch. From Eastern to Continental, you feel weak in forward power and can no longer punish a shoulder-high ball.

With an altered grip your wrist doesn't feel the same. With the new one it's sure to be less free for any last-second adjustment.

Continental and Eastern, the two most discussed grips and styles, clearly don't match.

Better Chances

You have a better chance with some of the others. The above difficulties apply to any alterations you make, but in lesser degree with more compatible grips. Forewarned, you may decide to experiment at least.

Continental to Australian—altering because your forehand is physically weak. You'll at once have a better topspin forehand from a higher ball, such as a topspin crosscourt service return in doubles from a shoulder-high ball in the right court. In singles you probably won't have the same control of length with your approach shots, without your fully accustomed feel for these. Whenever you play badly, you'll miss the strength of grip that the Continental grip's heel of the hand flat on the flat top surface of the handle gives you. If you alter back to Continental in mid-set, be sure to take the ball farther back beside your body once more, or your open racket face will loft the ball and you'll feel you've got nothing at all on the forehand side.

Extreme-Eastern to Eastern—altering because you want your forehand grip to be closer to an adequate backhand grip, so you won't be so lop-sided in strength. Since the grips and styles are similar, both giving a strong forehand that keeps the ball down well, you shouldn't have much trouble with your forehand and you'll achieve a better backhand. You'll lose some of your forehand flair though.

Semi-Western Style or Western Grip (both with Non-Western Backhands), to Extreme-Eastern or Eastern—altering for more forward speed (less looped topspin) and wider reach and a closer grip to your backhand for less lop-sidedness. To feel safe without your former heavy topspin you'll need to concentrate on longer forward contact together with forward topspin. You should achieve all your objects, but again lose some of your forehand flair.

Semi-Western Style or Western with Western Backhand, to Extreme-Eastern with Western Backhand—altering for more forward speed. This should be the least disruptive alteration that anyone could make.

With all alterations of forehand grip, only trial and error will show whether the change has been for the better, all round, or not. One hears of players' grips and styles being altered and their games ruined, but that will not apply to you if you completely give up an alteration and whole-heartedly go back to your original way of playing. You won't have improved meanwhile, but that's about all you need lose. Start again from where you left off, as though you hadn't played for a long time and without hankering after some of the alteration's better points that you now forgo.

Drastic Change

Western with Western Backhand, to Eastern, Australian or Continental—altering because you're tired of laboring with looped topspin and of court-covering with your legs instead of having a wider reach. Eastern will need an unaccustomed large change of grip for your backhand (a change made in a different direction too), and Continental (and to a lesser extent Australian) is a totally different concept from Western. Probably your best course is to use a Continental grip as a special shot for wide balls and to keep your Western strength for closer ones.

Pointless Alterations

Australian to Continental, Eastern to Australian, and perhaps Western to Semi-Western. It's hard to see advantage over your present naturalness.

BACKHAND

Official Classifications

The Continental being more or less a no-change style, the forehand grip shown in Illus. 54 with V on left bevel is also a Continental backhand grip. The inner edge of the thumb is often advanced diagonally across the back of the handle for support, other users preferring to leave the thumb around the handle for strength of grip. The Continental backhand grip is most flexible and is adequate in strength.

An Eastern backhand grip is shown in Illus. 25, the height of the base knuckle of the little finger showing that the hand is farther behind the handle than in the Continental grip. In the Eastern grip, the V reaches the back of the handle, and the thumb, advanced by most players, lies across the back of the handle less diagonally than in the Continental. The grip is most adequate in strength and sufficiently flexible.

A Western backhand takes the ball well in front of the body and uses the same racket face as the forehand to hit it. The grip is made from the forehand by turning the racket head in a semi-circle from right to left over and around the wrist, slightly adjusting the grip for comfort as necessary. The V lies on the back of the handle and the thumb is left wrapped around. The grip is more than adequate in strength and is inflexible.

Backhand Confusion

Some Continental players like to make a very small change for the backhand, for added pressure, and in so doing take an Eastern backhand grip. More significantly, most Eastern players don't change grip by 90° all the way round to an Eastern backhand, and so take a Continental backhand grip—understandably causing many people to regard this backhand as being Eastern, and then to think of the Eastern backhand used by some Continental players as being the real Continental one—perhaps. Except that that means calling a no-change Continental player's Continental backhand an Eastern, and that can't be right. Perhaps . . .

No wonder two people use the same name and mean two different grips.

The backhand used by most Eastern players must remain classified as Continental since it belongs to the Continental no-change style, but rather than argue further it is simpler to turn to more practical names. As styles are named from their forehand grips it doesn't matter if some other kind of name describes the backhand side. In fact, it's better. It's only a hindrance to have the same name for a forehand and its official backhand when so often the grips that players use don't officially match.

Descriptive Classifications

Adequate

Continental, more flexible.

Eastern, stronger.

Inadequate—See Illus. 26.

Any make-shift grip and method.

Eastern and Australian forehand grips used as backhand grips—since these don't give much strength even when the stroke is made as well as possible by holding the wrist low and back.

Inflexible

Eastern backhand grip with fingers bunched and the ball of the thumb run straight up the back of the handle.

Western backhand grip.

SERVICE

Your serve is best made like a throw that makes full use of the wrist at delivery. The term used is wrist-snap.

Your serve is made on your forehand side and hit with the forehand face of your racket—and the Continental forehand grip (not some backhand grip or other, with the thumb taken away) is the best grip to use for anyone who can manage it.

Look at a ball held in your fingers ready to throw, and regard your grip of it as your Continental forehand service grip (you· don't throw backhand). Hold your racket handle halfway up or more so that a few inches of it project below your wrist, and make simulated serves with Western, Extreme-Eastern or Eastern grips and note how the handle is in line with your wrist and interferes with it. With a Continental grip it does not.

Used at full length, this handle-free service grip allows you full wrist-snap for speed or twist. For the latter, see the Topspin serve in Illus. 10, where the racket head is being whipped upwards with full wrist-snap.

Render Unto Caesar

A Continental player would feel almost malformed if he thought he was playing his forehand with his backhand grip and a Continental-grip volleyer would feel his forehand volley to be second class. Like a throw, your service is on your forehand side—so serve with a forehand grip and don't inhibit yourself.

VOLLEYING

The best grip is the no-change Continental, if you can manage it on forehand as well as backhand. However, effectiveness comes first. For various suggestions see Volleying Grips.

OPPONENT'S STYLE

You can't see your opponent's grip and all its defining niceties 20 yards or so away at the other end of the court. It's his resulting style you see—can't help seeing—and from that you can be well prepared for the shots he's likely to have.

You won't have trouble recognizing types of players if you play practice sets and devote about three or four games in each to playing in each style yourself. You can play quite well in any style, when you're only practicing. Feel and see in your mind's eye what you look like, and thus what anyone else's strokes will look like to you.

Going from recognition to strengths and weaknesses, from a Continental grip see how easy it is to reach a wide ball and how difficult to hit a high one for a winner. Try changing from an Eastern forehand grip to an adequate backhand grip against a fast first serve, and move about the court carrying a two-handed backhand along with you. All your opponents have their troubles—to be exploited.

General Rules

Continentals look dextrous when they're good—and when they're not they seem to lack power on the forehand or to be erratic with it. Australians look sound all-around—or not severe enough anywhere. Easterners have solid pace from thigh height and above—or are too ponderous. Extreme-Easterners have a shoulder-high king hit—or the backhand hinders them.

Too pigeon-holed to be true? Well, when a Continental is clumsy and likes high forehands, or an Eastern is much stronger on the backhand, or a left-hander's best shot is a topspin cross-court backhand, or a two-handed player has a telescopic reach with his two-hander—you'll notice them.

APPENDIX 2

BALL CONTROL

The twin pillars of ball control are long contact and spin. Luckily, they act together, conscious long contact including some automatic spin and intentionally applied spin including some automatic long contact.

LONG CONTACT

When you've timed a ball well, don't let it go too soon; hold it, making the most of your timing. When playing an awkward shot that you can't time well, make up for that by holding the ball on the strings so that it's yours to control for as long as possible. And when you hit hard, which means that your shot has less margin for error, hold the ball as long as possible for control.

The advantage of long contact is obvious for your ground-strokes, serve and followed-through half volley, but the advantage holds for every shot where you have time for long contact. Your smash is safer for it. In a fast volleying exchange, you might stab at a couple of quick balls, and then up comes the easy one. Stabbing again, you can miss it, but putting it away with long contact, you can't. Notice that leading players follow this technique.

NOTE: Until you reach the heading, Spin on Other Strokes a few pages further on, the discussion below applies mainly to forehand groundstrokes.

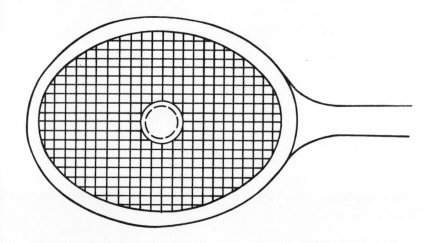

Illus. 59. FLAT DRIVE WITH CONSCIOUS LONG CONTACT. Feel that you have flattened the ball as shown. This makes you hit along the exact line that you should hit. When you do that, you're "on" the ball (racket face in line with it) for longer than with other types of forehand; also, your racket face is square when it hits the ball. On both counts you have every chance of contacting the ball cleanly, and you will hit it well.

From all this, feel that your flat drive can be a safe shot when used against a suitable ball, and not that it is always a risky shot because it needs a lower net clearance than a topspin forehand.

Flat Forehand

Long contact is most easily understood with a flat forehand drive, where it has its greatest effect. (See Illus. 59–60.)

On the matter of length, many players equate a flat drive with risk, because it may land just out, and a topspin forehand with safety, because it will drop just in. But the more topspin you put on a ball the more looped its flight is, and so the less certain you are of exactly where it will land. Also, the more spin you apply the less certain you are of how much it is. If you're aiming for depth using a lot of topspin, your shot may not have as much spin as you thought, and it, not the flat one,

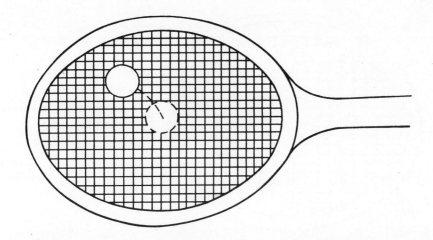

Illus. 60. BOGUS FLAT DRIVE. Don't dare call a shot you've made a flat drive just because you didn't put any topspin on it. That's a hit, no more; a flat hit, if you insist, but certainly no more than that.

lands just out. If it has more spin than you thought, it's not deep at all and you haven't put the ball behind your opponent, if that was your intention. Perhaps he can pelt it and take charge. The long-contact flat drive, through its accuracy, can be the safer shot.

Automatic Forward Spin

Besides long contact there is a slight built-in safety factor in the flat drive, and it adds to your confidence to be aware of it. The ball has a small amount of topspin on it (think of it as Forward Spin). You hit the ball with a flat racket face, but during your long contact your racket starts to rise a little in its swing and this small amount of lift imparts some forward spin to the ball. It's definitely there.

So that you're perfectly clear about this, it is an exaggeration for anyone to state that such-and-such a past champion always hit his forehand drive so flat that the brand on the ball always

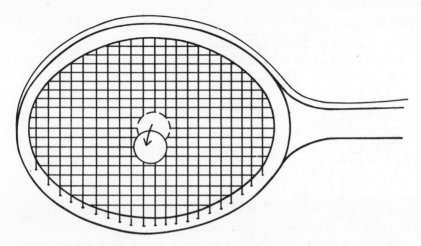

Illus. 61. TOPSPIN LONG CONTACT. Your topspin control increases when you use conscious long contact as well.

appeared to be stationary. It's not possible. Such drives would have to be hit with a modicum of underspin, which exactly offsets the forward spin automatically implanted by the lifting racket. On occasion a fairly short ball bouncing above net height can probably be driven downwards dead flat, but that's about all.

Rising-Ball Play

Likelihood of clean hitting, as indicated in Illus. 59, is a great advantage in rising-ball play. Like playing flat, playing on the rise is not all risk, as some players imagine, because you're compensated for the early stroke by having the best chance of taking the ball at the height you like best, without having to retreat to do so.

The advantages gained from rising-ball play are that if you meet the ball about 18 inches earlier than at the top of its bounce or just below it, you probably gain about double that distance, about a yard, on your opponent, and secondly that you get a most effective attack with little effort. Hold your racket firmly, but never in a grip of iron. (An overtight grip stiffens your backswing and commits the direction of your forward swing too early. For safe and competent rising-ball play, you need to be flexible enough to adjust for an unexpected bounce or to make a last-second change of direction.) Don't lean back just because the ball's coming up; lean forward and meet it, deliberately cutting its bounce short.

Flat rising-ball play is all a pipe-dream though, if you don't play it compactly and with ball control from solidly-felt long contact, and with your head dropped over the ball to see it clearly into your racket.

Topspin and Underspin Long Contact

A topspin drive includes an automatic form of long contact, whether its user knows it or not, because the ball rolls fractionally down your short strings before leaving the racket face. (See Illus. 61.)

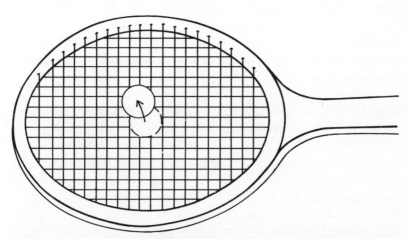

Illus. 62. UNDERSPIN LONG CONTACT. The ball slides slightly up the cross strings, giving a clinging feeling. Conscious forward long contact adds to your control, and the stroke is shorter and more easily made than a drive. It seems to be as safe as a stroke can be—but the racket face isn't square, and cutting sharply against fast balls leads to mis-hitting.

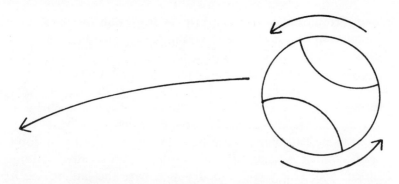

Illus. 63. TOPSPIN. The upper half of the ball bites into the air and so the ball must curve downwards if you've hit it properly. Should your own top-spin be weak, concentrate on hitting the ball strongly across your short strings. Imagine, if you like, that they're knotted around the main ones, giving you a cluster of little lumps to spin the ball from. **MAKE** it spin.

It's the same thing, in the other direction, with a cut or slice. (See Illus. 62 on previous page.)

General Rule

Long contact has a lot in common with ball-watching: it needs to be part of your game; it's natural to some extent, but is more effective when consciously done; and if you can't think of it all the time you should do so with the most appropriate shots. With ball-watching, appropriate shots are either your least reliable shot or your forehand side; with long contact it's again your least reliable shot or it's your longer shots—ground-strokes and service.

Long contact gives a feeling of firmness, control and safety. It is the essence of soundness, which is the essence of match play. Realize early in a game that if your opponent can't stop you from playing ball after ball with long contact, you'll win.

But if you think of nothing else you'll be slow. Further, it doesn't give you complete ball control; often you need to control the ball's flight mainly by spin, intentionally applied.

TOPSPIN

After hitting deeply with flat or only slightly rolled drives, masters of change of pace merely use a slower ball to play a short crosscourt angle or to find a volleyer's feet, but everyone else relies directly on topspin. Topspin makes the ball drop. (See Illus. 63.)

Since every shot in tennis has to go forward you mainly hit the back of the ball, but you can make much better use of its surface than that. Driving from behind the baseline, feel you're hitting slightly below the center of the ball (not halfway down, or you'll never control it) and lift on the spin, so that the ball's line of flight rises a little from your racket. In driving a ball that lands near the service line and bounces higher than the net, hit it slightly above center and make the ball spin downwards as part of its downward line of flight from your racket. They *feel* like two different shots, but in each the direction of spin and its axis are the same. (See Illus. 64.)

Illus. 64. TOPSPIN BACK VIEW. The direction of the spin is the same, whether you lift on topspin from below or roll it on from above. The forward spin of the ball ought to make it bounce lower than a flat ball, but its steeper drop more than offsets this. The combined effect of drop and forward spin makes your topspin drive bounce higher and longer than a flat drive.

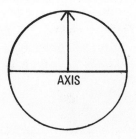

Illus. 65. OUTSIDE-TOPSPIN. The main effect is a downward topspin curve and a high and long bounce. The outside-spin component is small, but with a fast rolled ball it has an appreciable going-away effect on the bounce of a crosscourt drive. Even a player who normally likes to hit his crosscourt drive straight from hip to hip often has no time to line up perfectly and so needs to hit outside the ball to crosscourt it.

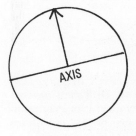

When you drive crosscourt and hit slightly outside the ball, the spin is mainly topspin but with a small amount of outside spin. (See Illus. 65 on previous page.)

Topspin Forms

Whether you're a left- or right-handed topspin player who never uses a flat drive because it doesn't suit your natural action and ball-control feel, don't play your singles matches using the same amount of topspin all the time. That's pick and shovel tennis. You hit heavily up and over the ball and drive it from corner to corner and have your opponent going from side to side—but you're the one who gets tired out.

And if you hit the ball higher and higher over the net to get depth because your topspin drops short, and if you then have to cram on more and more topspin to bring these higher and higher balls down again, and if all this goes on and on—you must get mentally tired out too.

Play your rallies with roll; hit fast short angles, or dip your shots against a volleyer, with topspin; and hit yourself out of

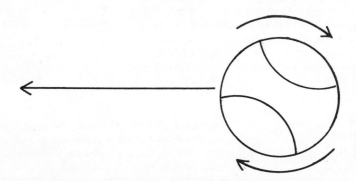

Illus. 66. UNDERSPIN. At speed, the lower side has enough friction against the air to work against gravity and keep the ball up. With shots near the baseline or sideline you can count on getting more bad luck than good. Your shot sails fairly straight above the ground and is easy to volley if within a volleyer's reach. Nevertheless, underspin has its other uses.

trouble with heavy topspin. Mis-hits will warn you of excessive topspin—which you correct with no loss of control by using less topspin and watching the ball better.

UNDERSPIN

Though underspin is always associated with control, it works the wrong way with forward speed near the lines; underspin keeps the ball *up*. (See Illus. 66.)

Backspin. Use a little assisting backspin to lift a low ball over the net with a horizontal racket, and use more for a drop shot. (See Illus. 67.)

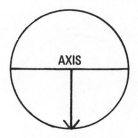

Illus. 67. BACKSPIN. This is pure underspin, though you don't mind if your shot includes a little sidespin. With strong backspin, the ball hangs in the air, bouncing noticeably more upright than a flat ball.

Outside-Underspin. Made from a low or medium ball, there is little sidespin and your shots swerve little. These shots are cuts for safety or to absorb speed, slices for more speed or good depth, and chip-approach shots to follow in behind. All have more underspin and less sidespin than you may think. (See Illus. 68.)

Illus. 68. OUTSIDE-UNDERSPIN. The sidespin component is slight. When attacking your opponent's forehand corner, these shots do not go away in curve or bounce as much as their opposite numbers (made with inside-underspin) go away from the backhand corner.

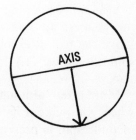

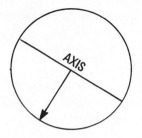

Illus. 69. INSIDE-UNDERSPIN. Sidespin component is greater than that of outside-underspin. Make use of it to the backcourt, but beware of it when making a passing shot. See Illus. 29 again.

Inside-Underspin. From low and medium balls underspin shots are more strongly made with inside spin. Make use of this extra swerve and going-away tendency to the backhand corner. Use plenty of swerve with your slider forehand—see Illus. 24 again. (Also see Illus. 69.)

Illus. 70. UNWANTED SPIN. It's only a trace, but it's in the opposite direction to even the small forward spin on a flat drive. It's enough to make the ball easy to volley and it ruins your short crosscourt drive as a passing shot.

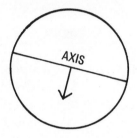

Unwanted Inside-Underspin. Don't play your forehand drive by dragging your elbow in towards your ribs, or, like many a stiff-wristed Continental player hitting to his off side, you will get unwanted or unnoticed inside-underspin on the ball, even though you may think you're hitting it flat. (See Illus. 70.)

Sidespin. Chopping strongly down on a high ball gives you the greatest amount of sidespin available. If you happen to strike the ball at exactly the right height you'll have pure sidespin. (See Illus. 71.)

More often, although the ball is still high (but not as high as when you make a half-smash or a sliced serve), some amount of underspin is present in your chop. (See Illus. 72.)

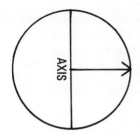

Illus. 71. PURE SIDESPIN. This produces a roundhouse curve that goes away across your opponent's forehand side or passes him down the line from wide out. See Illus. 27–28 again.

Illus. 72. MORE USUAL SIDESPIN. Your chop is still a sidespin shot and has a roundhouse curve.

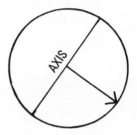

Underspin Use and Misuse

Use underspin for ball control, stroke-range and baseline corner penetration, but don't base your forehand on it. It doesn't provide enough speed against your opponent when he's at the baseline, and at the net he feeds on it.

SPIN ON OTHER STROKES

Backhand Spin

The variations of backhand underspin are not difficult to follow. Your backhand is strong from a short crosscourt swing, so backhand outside-underspin has stronger sidespin than the forehand. It matches forehand inside-underspin, combining with it to give you a penetrating attack to a right-hander's backhand corner.

Similarly, weaker backhand inside spin matches forehand outside spin and combines to give you a less penetrating attack to a left-hander's backhand corner. Realize this and use more weight.

From a high ball, no downward backhand chop is as strong as the forehand, which is able to make use of a longer swing.

For baseline rallying and passing shots, the backhand slice is stronger than the forehand. If your normal game has a rolled forehand and sliced backhand it's in much better balance than the reverse.

Sliced Service Spin

The main component is sidespin. (See Illus. 73.)

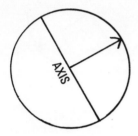

Illus. 73. SLICED-SERVICE SPIN. The main component being sidespin, the ball swerves and bounces going away, the bounce being lower than that from a flat ball. Compared with a downward chop, the ball is hit from higher up, and the other component is now topspin.

Although the topspin component is smaller, it is coupled with your downward service action and the downward flight path of the ball and thus has a strong effect. Throughout a match or the whole social afternoon many players take aim but send fast first serves down into the net.

Sidespin curve and topspin drop combine to give your serve more chance of landing in court, once the ball has passed the net; that's why you use them. But realize clearly that before the ball has passed the net they're combined against you.

Players use different concepts. Some say it's up to them to get the ball past the net, and then the swerve and drop land it in for them. Others concentrate on following through to give the ball the swerve and drop it needs to land in. Others serve a roundhouse sinker from start to finish. Some take little notice of spin, serving with long contact and feeling they're putting the racket head into the service court.

Whatever it is, have some basic concept to fall back on when you're not serving well. Don't make it this one: "I throw the ball up and hit it hard, and with its downward angle it ought to land in," or you'll put your fair share of fast first balls down in the net, all through the match, all social afternoon.

Topspin Serve

Here you roll on your topspin with an upward action and there's no downward net trap. Spin components and effects are seen in Illus. 74.

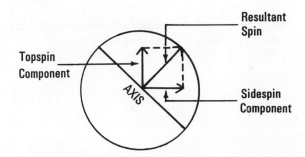

Illus. 74. TOPSPIN-SERVICE SPIN. The sidespin component curves the ball to your opponent's right, the topspin component making it drop sharply and bounce high and long. The direction of the resultant spin makes the bounce break back to the receiver's left—bounce is opposite to curve.

Topspin Sliced

Actions vary. If yours is upward you won't notice the net. If downward, remember that this serve allows you to have a fairly high net clearance.

Volleying Spin

Use underspin mostly. It helps to lift low volleys and also provides its automatic small measure of long contact when you've no time for conscious long contact.

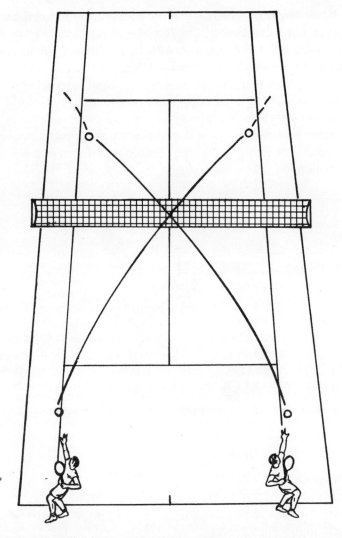

Illus. 75. LEFT- AND RIGHT-HANDED SERVICES. In the diagram, spin and curve look the same, but they don't on the court. The left one's to your backhand, but probably its unusualness has the greater effect. You'd swear it was wider.

Be aware that for low and medium volleys, you get stronger inside-underspin than outside-underspin for the forehand and the reverse for the backhand, and that for high volleys you get stronger outside-sidespin for both.

A stroke volley, made with roll from a short backswing against a suitably high ball, is a strong way to volley if it suits your game—though many right-handers have lived their lives through without having played one in a match.

Spin on Lobs

Mostly, hit flat or use underspin to attack from a good position, and use topspin to attack from a poor one—where you're trying to turn defeat into victory and don't mind the risk.

Smashes

The strong downward tendency of your smash is the most controlling factor you have; mainly, if you hit the ball over the net it will go in.

Spin does not play a great part—though if your normal serve is sliced you will naturally smash with some sidespin, and if it is topspin you'll smash towards your off side with a trace of that. In either case, whenever you're handling a high lob it's safer to feel you're using a full-faced racket than to feel anything else.

LEFT-HANDED SPIN

Although a left-hander probably gets no more spin and curve than a right-hander does on occasion, it doesn't feel that way to an opponent on court, where it counts. (See Illus. 75.)

Left-handers use spin more often. Having found it to be effective against right-handers they specialize in it and make it their natural game. Many would sooner hit a ball from A to B by any means other than using a straight line.

Most left-handers' spin is strong outside topspin for the forehand, relatively weak inside-underspin for the backhand

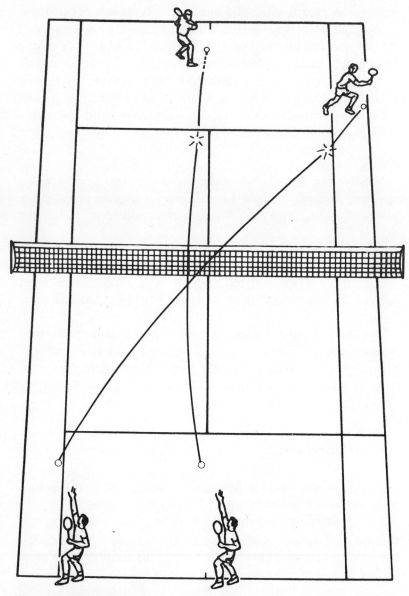

Illus. 76. (see opposite page).

and fairly strong topspin for the service. The groundstroke spins almost certainly result from early-days doubles play in the left court and the topspin-direction serve probably from having first learned to serve from the right side, along with everyone else, and serving the ball away to the off side.

Expect a left-hander to play the net game if he has a good serve. If it's topspin he'll use it to jam you—but at least the ball bounces high enough for you to have a downward angle for your passing shots.

Facing the worst case: he has a fast and swinging sliced serve that keeps low and which he follows in; a crosswind is favoring him; you have an underspin backhand. (See Illus. 76.)

You're against left-handed spin, all right.

Illus. 76. (opposite page) LEFT-HANDER'S SLICED SERVICE. To your right court, he advances behind the Center Theory, allowing you the least angle for a passing shot. To your left court, he doesn't serve from as far out as shown—but that's what his crosswind angle feels like. He swings the ball left-handedly wide, and you're underspinning a low ball back against half of the crosswind's force. You're not as close in as shown, either— that's where you'd like to be, if you had time to get there.

INDEX

playing the points 134-136
preferred direction 27-29
rallying 107
receiver, doubles 163-173
  attack 163-173
  back 170
  net barrier 164, 167-170
receiver's net man 159-162
  average 161
  strong partner 159-161
  weak 161
receiving serve 101, 103-107, 129-130, 163-164
  all-court player, against 105-107
  choosing to 129-130
  fast 163-164
  net player, against 101, 103-104
right-side collapse 65
rising ball 122, 163-164, 192-193
  grip 122
safety margin 107-108
salvaging your game 144-147
self-pity 15
Semi-Western 74
serve 13, 33-41, 99-100, 129-133, 141-144, 152-157, 186-187, 201
  American Twist 35, 38, 39
  ball position 33-39
  cannonball 37, 38, 39, 142-144
  doubles 152-157
  flat 37, 38, 39
  grip 40, 186-187
  left-handed 40-41
  second 13
  sliced 34-35, 36, 39, 99-100, 132
  timing 141
  topspin 35, 37-38, 99, 100, 133, 201
  topspin sliced 33, 34, 35, 36, 39, 133, 201
seventh game 136-137
short balls 66-67, 92
sideline clearance 107
sidespin 198, 199
slider forehand 68
smash 58-63, 142
  keys 147
  spin 203
  timing 61, 142
spin 190-205
spinning for serve 129-131
stalling 149-150
string areas 13, 14

sun 131-133
tandem 171-173
telegraphy 26
temper 15
temperament *see* match temperament
timing 140-142
timing pause 140-142
topspin 54-55, 146, 195-197
  forms 196-197
  keys 146
trouble, hitting out of 112
trouble, isolating 145-146
trumped ace 94-95
two-hander, playing against 85-86, 117
  backhand 85
  forehand 85-86
  types 117
two-stage advance 18
underspin 197-199
vertical racket 48-49, 53, 57
volley 12-13, 18, 21, 42-52, 161-162, 187, 201, 203
  angle 50
  backhand 42, 43, 46, 49
  depth 50
  first 18, 44-45
  grip 43-44, 45, 46-47, 48, 49
  high 12-13, 48, 49
  keys 147
  low 45-46
  medium 47-48
  racket position 42-43, 48-49
  second 18
  short 21
  spin 201, 203
  stroke 49
  wide 18, 46-47
warm-up 90, 122, 127-129, 144-145
watching the ball 15, 138-139, 146
Western grip 44, 46, 179
Western style, playing against 73-74
  forehand only 73
  Semi-Western 74
  two-handed 73-74
will to win 15
wind 68, 97, 116, 133-134
  crosswind 69, 97
  down-wind 116, 133
  gusts 134
  serving 133-134
wrist, free 134

208 ○ FINE POINTS OF TENNIS